CW01459221

ANNA CAM.. ____

Good Girl
Rebellion

Build the business,
break the rules,
be limitless

R^ethink

First published in Great Britain in 2025 by Rethink Press (www.rethinkpress.com)

© Copyright Anna Campbell

All rights reserved. No part of this publication may be reproduced, stored in or introduced into a retrieval system, or transmitted, in any form, or by any means (electronic, mechanical, photocopying, recording or otherwise) without the prior written permission of the publisher.

The right of Anna Campbell to be identified as the author of this work has been asserted by her in accordance with the Copyright, Designs and Patents Act 1988.

This book is sold subject to the condition that it shall not, by way of trade or otherwise, be lent, resold, hired out, or otherwise circulated without the publisher's prior consent in any form of binding or cover other than that in which it is published and without a similar condition including this condition being imposed on the subsequent purchaser.

To you.

The past doesn't define you.

Being good doesn't serve you.

Without it, you're limitless.

Jess

Thank you for everything. This
book wouldn't exist without you

Anna

Contents

Introduction   1

PART ONE   The Good Girl   7

1 What Is The Good Girl Personality?   9

   Why is it important to understand
   your personality?   10

   The Good Girl at school   12

   The four Good Girl personality traits   13

   Summary   21

2 Why Are We Like This?   23

   Nature versus nurture   24

   Free will versus determinism   29

   Historical context: Women,
   work and business   33

   Summary   35

3 The Good Girl's Guide To Getting
   Things Done   37

   Your motivation   38

   Why can't we 'just do it'?   40

The fallacy of my vision of my ideal self   41

Building your morning ritual   43

The answer hiding in plain sight   44

Getting things done   47

I can't 'just do it' – The paradox   53

Summary   55

4 Your Offer   **57**

Your vision (and why it's OK if you don't have one)   57

The products/services you need in your business   63

What to do if you're not making any money   65

Summary   67

PART TWO   The REBEL Methodology   **69**

5 Resilient Mindset   **71**

All business issues are mindset issues   73

How we deal with fear   77

Imposter syndrome   80

Self-sabotage   81

The transformational power of gratitude   84

Summary   86

6 Everyday Action   **87**

Decision-making   89

Managing your time   90

Boundaries   94

Productivity and seasons 100

Summary 102

7 **Bold Marketing** **105**

Locus of control 107

Time to unleash your inner diva 108

Your message 110

Where to share your message 113

Data-led decision-making 116

Developing your sales mindset 117

Summary 118

8 **Empowered Pricing** **121**

Your money mindset 122

The gender pay gap in self-employment 127

Why do we undercharge? 128

How to price correctly 130

Summary 133

9 **Liberating Results** **135**

It's time to get strategic 136

Goal setting 139

Dealing with setbacks 144

When should I give up the day job? 145

Summary 148

PART THREE **The Good Girl Leader** **151**

10 **Mistakes, Myths And Momentum** **153**

Support 155

Vision and clarity   157

Action   158

Giving up   160

Feeling stuck   161

Self-promotion   162

Visibility   163

Comparison   164

Failure   165

Success   166

Summary   167

11 Becoming The Good Girl Leader   169

Where are you holding yourself back?   171

Are you hyper independent?   173

In whose interest is it that you go it alone?   176

Summary   182

Conclusion   183

References   187

Further Reading   195

Acknowledgements   197

The Author   201

Introduction

Let me guess, you've spent your life doing what you should, being the dependable, capable one, working hard behind the scenes to ensure everyone else looks good and making other people money while putting your own dreams on the back burner. You make it look effortless while falling into bed exhausted every night. If you're tired of being the best-kept secret in your life, it's time for your Good Girl Rebellion.

Rebellion isn't about working harder; you're already busy enough. It's about rebelling against the outdated rules and systems that have been keeping you stuck. The truth is, you don't need to do more or change who you are, because you're brilliant. You just need a system that works *with* your personality not against it.

I know what it's like to feel stuck; to know there's something more you're meant to do but to have no clue how to make it happen. I was employee number one for a start-up. I did all the jobs and learnt how to grow a successful business from the inside. The business grew to seven-figure years, and I was a big part of that growth, but when it came to my own business I froze. I spent time over-planning, over-analysing and drowning in advice from gurus who were not like me, and I ended up no closer to building my own dream business.

That's when it hit me: I wasn't the problem; the problem was the rules I'd been following. The strategies that made me a brilliant employee were holding me back as an entrepreneur. I needed a different approach.

I went back to what I'd learnt studying and teaching psychology (I had previously been a lecturer at a London university). I rewrote the rules and started managing myself in a way that worked for my personality. Everything changed.

In this book, I bring my background in psychology and as a Wayfinder life coach to look at the mindset and behavioural side of our personalities and businesses. I bring my experience of running my own oversubscribed business as well as growing a million-pound-a-year business, specialising in marketing, where I regularly wrote emails that made tens of thousands. I also bring my certification as a sales strategist and a perspective that I haven't seen in business books, focusing only on our personality types – this book is not for everyone.

I founded the Good Girl Rebellion to help women like me grow their own businesses. In some ways, the stats are depressing, but they also show that there is space for women to build successful businesses, and change is already happening. In the UK, only one-third of entrepreneurs are women. When surveyed, 55% more women than men said that they feared starting a business alone and their perception was they lacked the skills and experience they felt they needed.[1] Don't worry, that's why this book and the Good Girl Rebellion exist. In the USA, the percentage of women entrepreneurs is similar: 39.2% of US businesses are owned by women, and this is reported as a significant growth from 2019 to 2024.[2]

On average, around 4% of businesses fail in the first year, 34% in the second year and 50% after three years.[3] It can take around three years for a business to become profitable. I don't say this to put you off but to encourage you to take the long view. The time will pass anyway, so why not spend it growing not just a business that you believe in, but a life lived on your own terms? There are things you can do to ensure you are in the thriving 50%, and this book is here to help ensure you do them.

This isn't just about building a business. It goes much deeper. It's about shedding your old skin, stepping into your power, writing your own story and being open to receive because you have been a giver for too long. You don't need another podcast, another guru, another to-do list. You need someone who truly gets it. Someone who's been there. Someone who can help you navigate the mindset blocks, the overwhelm and the fear that's keeping you stuck.

What's exciting is that this is a part of something big. This book is scattered with disruptive, rebellious ideas. It is your invitation to be part of a movement, a cultural shift. We have so much to offer; we need to stop shrinking ourselves to fit into outdated expectations and start stepping into our limitless power.

It's time to REBEL

We need to take the following steps to move from the Good Girl Great Employee to the Good Girl Rebel, fearless leader and successful entrepreneur:

- Resilient mindset – All business issues are mindset issues at their core so let's clear away blocks like overwhelm, indecision, imposter syndrome and fear of criticism so that we can be confident and ready for growth.

- Everyday action – We need to find the way to prioritise our businesses and get moving in the right direction. It sounds so simple but it is one of our biggest blocks to a successful business.

- Bold marketing – We're the ones who need to spread the word about our businesses, even if it doesn't come naturally at first. We need to find a way to do it, because staying quiet won't get us seen.

- Empowered pricing – Your money and selling mindset affects how you show up for your business. Women undercharge, and that has to stop.

- Liberating results – When we do the rest, success will follow.

If this has you nodding your head with agreement and wondering how I'm in your mind, it's because this is exactly what was in my head too. I needed my Good Girl Rebellion. It has been a profound shift in how I see and act in the world. It's like looking through a colourful kaleidoscope – one tiny turn and the whole picture changes.

The Good Girl Rebellion is for you if:

- You've tried to grow your business following someone else's rules and they're not working for you

- You're stuck in a never-ending cycle of overthinking, prioritising everyone else and not making money

- You're sick of working so hard, grinding away but never seeming to get anywhere

- Overwhelm happens when you don't have a system that works for you

- Fear is your Good Girl conditioning trying to keep you small

- You know it's time to truly be your limitless self

It's time for your Good Girl Rebellion.

PART ONE
THE GOOD GIRL

Let's begin with you because it's about time you came first. Your personality is a blend of powerful traits that hold your superpowers, but every strength also has a shadow side. The first step is truly understanding and owning who you are and how that plays into how you run a business. We'll dive into the psychology of why you think, act and react in the way that you do.

Next it's time for The Good Girl's Guide to Getting it Done. If you are beyond frustrated that you can prioritise everyone else's goals but for some reason struggle when it comes to your own, this chapter tells you why. There's a secret to consistently working towards your own goals without the use of willpower and it's been hiding in plain sight.

Finally, we'll bring it all together by looking at your offer. This book is for you whether you are a product-based or service-based business (I have worked with both). We'll refine the products you have, and I'll tell you which one most people will buy from you.

Ready to go? Let's do this.

1
What Is The Good Girl Personality?

The Good Girl personality is a series of traits that slot together like puzzle pieces. These traits make you look at the world and act in a particular way – your superpowers and your shadow side. In this chapter we will look at these traits, how they relate to the way you do business and how to harness who you are in your gorgeous imperfect perfection. In the next chapter, we'll delve into the psychology and look at why you have this personality.

EXERCISE: Do you have a Good Girl personality?

As with everything to do with our personalities and who we are, these traits are on a spectrum. You may identify that one trait is strong in you, while another is there but not as prominent. I suggest taking this free personality quiz, which will help clarify whether you have a Good Girl personality, www.goodgirlrebellion.com/book.

The key traits of the Good Girl personality are:

- **High empathy** – You are good at reading people and anticipating what they need.

- **High reliability** – When you commit to doing something for others you will see it through.

- **High integrity** – You have strong morals and will act on your beliefs in what is right and wrong.

- **Great collaborator** – You work well with others and they love having you on the team.

Why is it important to understand your personality?

Before we get into our traits in detail, let's take a step back to look at why this is so important. Understanding ourselves at a deeper level is the key to knowing how to motivate, manage and care for ourselves. The fact is, we are different from others, and we can end up on completely the wrong track when we look to the wrong people to be our role models for how to grow a business. I learnt this one the hard way, and that's why I created the Good Girl Rebellion.

My journey to this realisation has been anything but straightforward. Working for a successful start-up and being a part of it all gave me a false sense of security. I thought, 'I know what to do, I'll do it for myself.' Yet my own business fell flat until I had an 'aha' moment and realised just how different I was from my boss, Jess. Jessica Rose is a brilliant entrepreneur who I've been fortunate to work with for over a decade. As we've worked together closely, I can confidently say that she sees risk differently. She also plans her days differently. Her goals, her ambitions, her entire approach to business is nothing like mine. Jess is not a Good Girl Rebel. If I'm being honest, I've yet to meet a Good Girl Rebel solopreneur with a million-pound business. Not because we don't exist but because we're rare. (My dearest hope is that this book helps change that.)

Why are we rare? Because the traditional models of success – the webinars, the books (except this one!), the 'tried-and-true strategies' weren't built for us. We try to replicate them and stall out. Not because we're incapable, but because we're wired differently. It's time to do things *our* way.

Understanding our personalities and the way we see the world is fundamental to who we are. It is key to understanding the REBEL methodology and why it works for us.

The Good Girl at school

If you think back to the school classroom and get a bit stereotypical, we Good Girls were the ones listening fairly attentively, quietly getting on with our work and handing our homework in on time. Others were always asking questions and pushing the boundaries. Still others were the rebels, not turning up to class, not caring about authority figures and doing their own thing.[4]

Although we were respectful and got on with it, that does not mean we were angels. We were much more likely to get away with things because no one suspected us! In this case, the term Good Girl is used to reflect not just ourselves but also how others view us.

Why this matters

Our thoughts, behaviour and decisions stem from who we are as a person. The strengths we have are things we can build on, but the shadow side can become our blocks. The first step is to shine a light on your traits and be aware of how it all fits together. The more you recognise your own patterns – good and bad – the greater your opportunity to step into your potential.

The four Good Girl personality traits

The four key Good Girl personality traits hold both your superpowers and a shadow side that might unconsciously be holding you back.

EXERCISE: Your key traits

It's time for some journalling. You'll need a few pages for this exercise. At the top of each page, write the following traits:

1. High empathy
2. High reliability
3. High integrity
4. Great collaborator

As you read through the descriptions below, reflect on these questions:

- How does this trait show up in my life and my work?
- In what ways does this trait support my success?
- Are there any ways in which this trait has been creating challenges or limitations for me?

Write down your initial thoughts as you read and then put it to one side to let your unconscious mind work on it. I recommend doing this exercise again in a couple of days to see what fresh insights have come to you.

1. High empathy

Empathy is the ability to understand and connect with the emotions and experiences of others. Your empathy is likely high, which means that you are great at anticipating the needs of others, and that helps you build trust.

Empathy is your superpower because:

- **You have great product/service ideas** – You think deeply about what people want and need, so your ideas are well thought through.

- **You are great at problem solving** – You have a wide view and can think through the complexities and potential pitfalls to pre-empt them. You are a solution-oriented person.

- **You make a great leader** – People are motivated to do their best work for you because they know you care about them.

- **You are service-oriented** – You consider not just the products/services you provide but also the larger picture and how your customers feel.

The shadow side for you and your business:

- **You struggle with boundaries** – You find setting and enforcing boundaries around your time and energy difficult in both your professional and personal life. This can easily lead to feeling burnt out and used.

- **You have difficulty with pricing and negotiation** – You may think more about your customers and their ability to pay than your need to charge correctly (see Chapter 8).

- **You avoid hard conversations** – You don't want to hurt people's feelings and may avoid the difficult conversations with employees that you need to have.

- **You take criticism personally** – Negative feedback and criticism can be difficult to hear because the business feels so personal to you. This can also mean that you hold back on stepping forward in the way you need to when you have your own business.

- **You are slow to make decisions** – Overthinking is a consistent theme! You can see the big picture of all the ways something could be done and how you could make it work, which can lead to overwhelm, putting off making decisions and picking one path.

2. High reliability

In the context of your business, high reliability means you are consistent, dependable and trustworthy. You deliver on what you've promised.

Reliability is your superpower because:

- **You have trust and credibility** – You demonstrate time and again that you can be trusted and that has helped to build your credibility as a businessperson.

- **You are consistent with your customers/clients** – You can be relied upon to do what you say you will.

- **You are a dependable leader** – Your team knows they can depend on what you say, and they feel confident to work with you.

The shadow side for you and your business:

- **You struggle with delegation** – You may find that as your business grows, you struggle to delegate tasks, which can lead to you being a bottleneck for growth.

- **You are prone to perfectionism** – You want everything to be just so before you release a new product or share a new service. This will likely delay you and your progress.

- **You overcommit** – You are prone to say yes to too much for fear of letting people down and then struggle to keep up with the workload you create for yourself.

3. High integrity

Having high integrity means that you are honest. You value transparency and doing the right thing, even when no one is watching. You have strong moral principles and are committed to doing what's right, even if it's not the easiest or cheapest path.

Integrity is your superpower because:

- **You are loyal** – Your actions and interactions with people create loyalty and advocacy. This means they won't only be loyal to you, they will also recommend you to others – these recommendations are business gold dust.

- **You have sustainable business growth** – You make decisions based on your values and ethics, not just on short-term gain. This ensures that your business has longevity.

- **You have clear brand values** – You have clear values that you can share with your customers/ clients. These are part of your business DNA and people see that in all you do.

The shadow side for you and your business:

- **You struggle with boundaries** – Yes, this one raises its ugly head again! (There is a section on boundaries coming up in Chapter 6, so we can deal with this.)

- **You are overly self-critical** – You have high standards and may fall short from time to time, leading to self-criticism and doubt about doing the right thing.

- **You worry about affordability** – Pricing comes up again here as there can sometimes be a conflict between what your business is worth and what you feel able to charge.

4. Great collaborator

As a result of your high empathy, high integrity and high reliability, you are a great collaborator. You can use your skills to develop strong relationships and act as a connector to bring them together. You truly value other people's input and know that when we work together, we are greater than the sum of our parts.

Collaborating is your superpower because:

- **You can build strong relationships and partnerships** – You build great connections at all levels, including with your staff, your customers/ clients and external partners that you work with.

- **You build strong networks** – When you do network, you are all about the win-win. The people you meet love that energy and want to help you too.

- **You are great at working through creative solutions with others** – For example, if someone comes to you with an issue, you ask the right questions and help them look at things from different angles.

The shadow side for you and your business:

- **You are at risk of overcommitting** – You want to work with others and say yes to projects so are at risk of overcommitting and neglecting areas you need to work on in your own business.

- **You are slow at decision-making** – It is one thing to be a part of a management team and quite another to be the CEO of your own business. Being slow to make decisions slows down the growth of the business.

- **You prioritise others** – While being focused on others is a superpower, it can lead to giving and not being open to receiving. In business, we need to be ready to receive too.

Consequences of the Good Girl personality traits

Lack of self-care is a consequence of all of the traits mentioned so far. We can struggle to care for ourselves and our own energy because our focus is so often outwards with everyone else. This is a reminder that you are your biggest business asset. Caring for your own wellbeing, energy and health is not just important for you, it is fundamental to the success of your business. If you need an external reason to look after yourself, you have one!

MY STORY: The Courtesy and Thoughtfulness Prize

I went to a primary school (elementary school for my US friends) that had a Courtesy and Thoughtfulness Prize. The prize was given once a year to two people in the school, one for a student in years one to three and one for a student in years four to six. I won that prize twice. I can't even tell you why and what for. I suspect the reason is for all the traits that I have just listed. It certainly wasn't any guile or trying to win anything, it was a prize for just being myself! Were you ever awarded something like this?

I hope you can see how these personality traits come together to make you the astonishing person that you are. If there is a part of you that feels frustrated and just wants to change, trust me, I get it. I used to think I could get much further in business if I didn't care so much about others. I could move faster if I didn't get stuck in overthinking and struggling to make decisions. I wish I could be motivated by my own priorities and stop putting others first.

This is where the dance begins. We can get stuck in either/or thinking, but that doesn't have to be the answer. We can embrace who we are and choose to act differently. We have free will.

How do we do that? This is what this book is about. For now, I want to assure you of your brilliance and everything you have to bring to the world and your business. A powerful shift happens when you fully accept who you are and still want more, when you recognise that the mindset and habits you have now are not the ones that will get you to where you want to go.

Summary

- Our blend of personality traits makes us brilliant business people but also has a shadow side that affects our progress.

- The Good Girl personality traits are high empathy, reliability and integrity and being a great collaborator.

- Understanding ourselves is key to knowing how to manage and motivate ourselves.

- Many of the key business books and advice don't work for us because they are written by people with a fundamentally different personality.

- The term Good Girl is used to reflect not just ourselves but also how others view us.

- Lack of self-care is a consequence of all the Good Girl personality traits.

- In the next chapter we're going on a detour to understand more about our personalities and why we are wired like this in the first place.

2

Why Are We Like This?

A s humans, we are interested in how we tick and why we are who we are. I want to share a whistlestop tour of current thinking here; it can be helpful to know why we are who we are, as self-understanding is the beginning of self-compassion and self-management. I have always been fascinated by this, so much so that my undergraduate degree is in psychology and I also have a postgrad in the subject. There are many great books that go into depth about this subject; if you would like to deep dive into this topic, I share some resources to check out in the Further Reading section.

In this chapter we're going to look at what the psychologists and researchers theorise about where personality comes from, both in general and for our Good Girl traits specifically. We will think about whether we can change and whether being the Good Girl is actually a trauma response. I encourage you to read this chapter to gain a better understanding of yourself, even if you're chomping at the bit to get to the REBEL action steps.

Nature versus nurture

Let's take a step back and look at where your personality and behaviour patterns come from. One of the fundamental debates in psychology is nature versus nurture. This is balancing how much of who you are is your nature – your genetics, physical organs (including the brain), neurochemicals and hormones, etc – and how much is nurture – your culture, society, upbringing, schooling, life experience, etc. You won't be surprised to hear that you are a product of both nature and nurture and it's not as simple as saying it's a fifty-fifty split.

Inherited traits and genetics

How much of your personality is genetic? Research into this is, relatively speaking, still in the early stages. Historically, a lot of the research and conclusions came from twin studies. Identical twins are interesting because they share 100% of the same genes, so researchers love the opportunity to look at the similarities and differences between them. Studies of twins, for example that by Bouchard et al in 1990,[5] suggests that between 40% and 60% of personality traits are heritable. Let's stop right there for a second because that's a big deal. We know about physical things like eye colour being inherited, but personality? That's important to know.

A 2016 study of molecular genetics and personality by Plomin et al showed that it's not as simple as one gene being responsible for one element of personality, but that a pattern of genes together combine to create different personality traits.[6]

Environment

While our genetic make-up may be the blueprint of ourselves, our environment is also key to who we are. Just think for a moment. If you had been born exactly as you were to the same parents but 200 years earlier, how would your life be different? What if you were born in a different country with a different culture? Even with your genes being the same, your life experience would be radically different and so your personality would be different too.

We can now add in another layer of complexity: epigenetics. The study of epigenetics is looking into how your environment influences your gene expression, which will, in turn, affect your behaviour and personality. Right now, the researchers are looking into the effects of diet, exercise, stress, environmental factors like pollutants, and parental and early life experiences.

Once again, research into this is in its infancy and the focus of most of the research is not on personality, but there is some evidence to suggest that childhood trauma has been linked to changes in stress response and mental health.[7] This gives us an inkling into how our personality might also be shaped.

Why are we this personality?

When we look specifically at the Good Girl personality traits, there is some key research that sheds some light. As a short and sweet summary of some of the main findings right now:

- Twin studies by Bouchard et al have shown that 'agreeableness' and 'reliability' are somewhat inherited but also shaped by upbringing.[8]
- McQuaid et al have found a genetic link to higher sensitivity to social rejection and stress.[9]
- Kogan et al found a gene linked to prosocial behaviour, empathy and emotional sensitivity.[10]

All of this indicates that our genetic inheritance does play a part in shaping who we are.

When it comes to our environment, there is a lot of research showing the differences in the ways that girls and boys learn about expectations of them is based on their gender.[11,12,13,14] For me, this is obvious. While it's beyond the scope of this book to address how children should be raised, it's worth highlighting here because it is one of the reasons this movement is called the Good Girl Rebellion. Of course, men can have high empathy, high reliability and high integrity, but these traits are more prevalent in women, and upbringing appears to be a big cause of this.

Interestingly, there are studies that show personality traits including reliability and conscientiousness change as we age, so this is not something that is set.[15] The conclusions we can draw are that the interplay between our genetic inheritance and our environment is complex and key to who we are as a person.

I have seen discussion of high empathy being a traumatic response and, at its extreme, it certainly can be. An example is people that were raised in a household with domestic violence – to survive, children can become supremely tuned into the nuances of mood and good at reading people.[16] For the majority of us, it is a function of our upbringing and responding to the expectations of those around us.

EXERCISE: The making of me

Get your journal out and reflect on these questions for yourself.

A note before you get started. Please go gently with yourself and skip any questions that might bring up anything that could distress you. The intention here is better self-understanding, not to open up old wounds.

1. Which aspects of your personality feel like they have consistently been a part of you? For example, have you always been quiet, loud, dramatic, artistic, shy or curious?

2. How do you think your upbringing shaped how you are today? For example, were you told to be quiet, expected to care for siblings or taught to put others first?

3. Can you think of any traits that you have as a result of life experiences? Think about milestone moments that have affected you – schooling, work, challenges.

4. In what ways have you consciously tried to grow or change your personality traits? For example, have you worked on your confidence and assertiveness?

5. If you were raised in a completely different environment, what traits do you think you would still have and what might be different? You could consider a completely different socio-economic background, being born 200 years earlier or being raised in a different culture.

I hope this exercise gives you the chance for some deep reflection and a realisation of how amazing you are. We can get caught up on traits we have that feel negative or that we might perceive are

holding us back. Instead, we can be grateful for who we are and ready to be more.

Free will versus determinism

Another key debate alongside nature versus nurture is free will versus determinism. That is, how much of who we are is based on our own free will – our ability to think and act as we want – and how much is determined, for example by our biology and upbringing. The research into epigenetics and gene expression currently suggests that some environmental factors can influence whether a gene is switched on or off so the interplay of these is closer than had previously been thought.[17]

This is an interesting debate and I certainly believe in free will; we all get to decide how we act in any given moment. Yet, I see how our day-to-day decision-making and lives can be shaped by what I will call 'our programming' – our genetic predispositions, environment and upbringing.

Can we change?

One thing people who are dissatisfied with the way they are often ask is whether we can change.

Yes, we can change. There may well be something big that you have changed about yourself. Perhaps you've been able to change your diet and be more mindful about eating healthily. Perhaps when you were a child you sucked your thumb and now you don't. If you've ever set a New Year's resolution and not followed through on it you'll know how hard it is to make even the simplest change in one area of your life.

Change takes time and conscious effort to embed into your life. Key research on change found that the average amount of time it takes to change a habit is 66 days, with a range of 18 to 254 days depending on how complex the habit was to integrate into daily life.[18]

How do we change?

If you've decided you want to make a real change in your life, here are the steps:

1. **Have clarity.** Be completely clear about what the change you want to make is. Some changes are easier to define than others; for example, if you want to get up at 5am every day, it is easy to tick off whether you have achieved this or not. If your goal is to set clearer boundaries with people, for example, that is more difficult to be clear on, so setting your own parameters and rules is important.[19]

2. **Have a big enough 'why'.** Write out why this change is important to you and be as clear and emotive as possible. Read this every single day as this will help get you through when you are demotivated.[20]

3. **Identify yourself as the person that does the change.** Taking the getting up early example, you need to consistently tell yourself, 'I am an early riser.'[21]

4. **Make it easy to do it and hard not to.** Find ways to ensure that you make the change every single day. When rising early, it could be about setting multiple alarms, having an alarm go off in another room so you have to get up to switch it off, or getting an alarm clock that turns on the light.[22]

5. **Have rewards and consequences.** How can you reward yourself when you do it and find a negative consequence when you don't? Have these set up in advance and ruthlessly stick to them.[23]

6. **Set yourself up to succeed.** Often when we set a target, other things in life need to change. If getting up early is what you want to do, ensure you are going to bed earlier and getting good-quality sleep. That may mean avoiding caffeine after 2pm, for example.

7. **Track your success.** Find a way to keep a track of your progress, whether in a habit tracker, a calendar or a diary.[24]

8. **Embrace discomfort.** You need to expect that making any change to your behaviour is going to feel uncomfortable to start with (Senge, 1990).[25]

The key is to pick your battles. The Good Girl Rebellion is about freedom, not destruction. It is a shedding of expectations and the weight we carry on our shoulders. There is a subtle distinction I hope you will get through this book. There is nothing wrong with us; we just need to find a way to harness who we are and channel that into creating the successful business and life that we love, while also making some subtle changes if we find we need to.

If there is an aspect of who you are that you want to change, you can absolutely do it, but be strategic and mindful about what that aspect is, knowing that it is going to take daily decisions and constant recommitment to ensure you make it happen.

The Four Tendencies

My big 'aha' moment in terms of understanding myself and growing my business came when I read *The Four Tendencies* by Gretchen Rubin.[26] I had been trying to follow the advice of business gurus, reading books and watching webinars. Everything they said made complete sense to me but I was never able to implement the advice myself; it always felt so alien. I started to think that I didn't have what it took to build a business, despite knowing what to do and seeing a business grow from the inside. Gretchen Rubin's book opened my eyes to a new explanation. If you are interested in changing your habits, her books are fantastic and I highly recommend them.

She talks about four different tendencies when it comes to responding to inner and outer expectations. Inner expectations are your own personal goals; outer expectations are rules, deadlines and expectations from others. This was the first time I'd seen personality described in quite this way and it got me thinking.

I delved further into personality studies, looking at a wider context of personality traits with a slant on our ability to grow a thriving business of our own. From this I developed the REBEL methodology and tested it on myself, my group clients and my coaching clients. I hit on something I hadn't seen explained in this way before.

While talking about it with someone else (who is not a Good Girl personality), I could see that she was confused because it didn't resonate with her. When I said we were the Good Girls at school, the ones that got on with their work, didn't disrupt the lesson and handed our homework in on time, she could understand what I was talking about. That is when I started to use the term Good Girl personality to describe our pattern of traits.

Historical context: Women, work and business

It's important to consider the historical context of women running their own businesses and having their own finances. As someone born in the 1970s, I have seen a large amount of change in this in my lifetime. Every country has their own story. I've chosen the UK and USA as examples for their wealth of available research and as a snapshot of progress and challenge:

- **UK** (1975): The Sex Discrimination Act and Equal Pay Act came into effect, making it illegal to discriminate based on gender in employment and pay. This also covered the ability for women to apply for loans and mortgages without a male guarantor.

- **USA** (1974): The Equal Credit Opportunity Act (ECOA) was passed, allowing women to apply for credit cards, mortgages and loans without a husband or male co-signer. Before this, banks often required a male guarantor.

MY STORY: Changing times

I have also lived through changing times. When I went to university I did not have access to the internet. When I left, it wouldn't have crossed my mind that I could start my own business. I didn't know what to do so I ended up going back to work at the shop I had worked at while at university. To start a business at that time meant you needed a lot of money to invest and I did not have that, even if the idea had crossed my mind.

It is only in the last couple of decades that it has become easy to sell online and to start a business with little to no start-up money required, and social media means we can access a global audience. These changes mean that women in their twenties, thirties, forties, fifties and sixties now have more opportunities than ever for starting their own business. This is great news, but in many ways we are the pioneers finding our own way forward in an ever-changing landscape.

Summary

- The Good Girl personality traits are likely a result of both your genetics and your environment.

- Research shows the differences in the ways that girls and boys learn about expectations of them is based on their gender.

- At its extreme, high empathy can be a traumatic response.

- Key debates include nature versus nurture and free will versus determinism.

- To make a change, have clarity, have a big enough 'why', identify yourself as the person that does the change, make it easy to do it and hard not to, have rewards and consequences, set yourself up to succeed, track your success and embrace discomfort.

- While change is possible, it's important to pick your battles.

Let's look next at how we get things done to grow our profitable businesses.

3

The Good Girl's Guide To Getting Things Done

This chapter contains all the hard-won knowledge that has taken me decades to realise and fully appreciate. My hope is that you take it all in now and that it changes your life. Sounds like a bold statement. The thing is, you are likely reading this book motivated by one or all of these three reasons:

1. You identify with the Good Girl personality and are curious to know more about it.

2. You know you want to grow a business; you don't know what you need to do to get there.

3. There are things you know you should be doing but you can't make yourself do them.

In this chapter I am going to tell you how to do the things you know you want to do but for some reason you're not doing.

Your motivation

Let's start with understanding motivation. Motivation is so important but it can feel ethereal. One of the most comforting things I ever heard is that for anything, including our business, we are motivated about one-third of the time, unmotivated and a bit 'meh' another third of the time, and demotivated the final third of the time. I can end up second guessing myself when my motivation ebbs, wondering if I'm doing the wrong thing or if I'm wasting my time. Knowing this about motivation has helped me keep moving forwards, even in those moments.

There are different types of motivation, and understanding and harnessing your own unique blend is the key to longevity in business. Let's look at the differences between intrinsic and extrinsic motivation. Intrinsic motivation includes your own desires, values and passions. It is likely that these are part of your drive to grow your own business. Extrinsic motivation includes the external factors that push you forwards, such as financial reward, accolades and recognition.[27]

EXERCISE: Your motivation

It's time to get your journal out and reflect on your underlying motivations. There are no right or wrong answers here, just your answers. Be honest with yourself. Understanding exactly what is underlying your will to grow your business will help you to keep going in those times when your motivation is at a low ebb.

Answer the following questions on intrinsic motivation:

- What inspired you to start your business?
- Why are the products/services of your business important to you?
- How do your personal values align with your business goals?
- How important is it to have creative freedom in your business?

Now think about your extrinsic motivation:

- What does success look like to you from the outside?
- What would your successful business look like?
- What milestones would you like to achieve in your business?
- What role does financial independence play in your motivation to have a business?
- What external results motivate you most: profit or praise?

Once you have your answers to these questions, keep them safe. They are your blueprint for your will to grow your business and it is good to review them regularly.

Why can't we 'just do it'?

The Nike slogan 'Just Do It' is interesting because it sounds so simple and yet if it were, everyone in the world would be smashing their goals all of the time. Simple does not mean easy, but if we have free will why aren't we out there 'just doing it' all over the place?

What is annoying is that the maxim 'just do it' is enough for some people and they can't see why the rest of us can't do it too. In Gretchen Rubin's theory, these are the Upholders and the Questioners.[28] It's not that they don't work for what they have or that their achievements should be discounted, but their outlook and the ways they are motivated differ from ours and they don't understand why we aren't 'just doing it'. Neither do we, when it comes to it. We judge ourselves on the fact that we're unable to motivate ourselves that way, especially when many of the books and personal development programmes are written from the perspective of someone who does just that.

In the rest of this chapter, I'm going to share two different approaches to getting things done and I strongly suggest that you work on them both. They are going to seem in opposition – that's because they are in a lot of ways. In order to have real success we need to build our ability to 'just do it' while tapping into the ways that work right now for us to get things done.

One of the fundamental laws in physics is the law of inertia, which states that an object stays at rest unless something causes it to move. It is in our personality and our nature that external forces – the expectations from others and the external deadlines – are what move us to action. This is why having our own business can be a struggle against ourselves and our inertia. If your boss gives you a deadline you will always meet it. If you give yourself a deadline it doesn't have the same pull.

The fallacy of my vision of my ideal self

MY STORY: Coming to terms with my real self

I used to believe that one day I would wake up and be my ideal self. I'd be productive and use every waking hour with efficiency. I'd be decisive, make the right choices in every moment and not delay doing what I knew in my bones I wanted and needed to.

It has been a slow realisation that has shown me that this exacting and narrow definition is a ridiculous fantasy. I was holding myself to a high standard – an either/or. Either I was that ideal self or I was nothing and no one.

The truth is that I can drag my feet and get it done. I can rest and allow my subconscious to come up with the answer. I can still be my ideal self but my definition of it has changed and become more nuanced and forgiving, more real, and that has been freeing.

This is where the real work comes in. I don't want you to read this book and put it back on the shelf and do nothing. I want this to be the last book you read before everything happens for you. It truly can be if you take this in *and* you act.

The big question is this: if nothing was to change in your life, would you be happy? Would that be enough for you? If not, are you willing to commit to making the changes you need to ensure you have the life and the business you envisage? This is an important question because you need to be completely done with being stuck and ready to move now. Otherwise, the inertia will keep you pinned right here.

If you're ready to commit to yourself, read on. If not, I suggest coming back to this book when you are.

Building your morning ritual

The biggest game changer for me in terms of being able to stay motivated and move out of inertia is my morning commitment to focus on what I want to achieve. It is about leading myself first.

I enjoy creating my own morning ritual and I change it up periodically. I encourage you to find your own routine and words to make this have meaning for you. You can make this fit the time that you have – I would suggest a minimum of fifteen minutes, but if you can do half an hour that is great. The following is the structure that works for me (for those who are interested in the specifics of my current morning practice, check out goodgirlrebellion.com/book):

1. **Your rebel anthem (5 minutes).** Find a song that encapsulates your rebellion, put it on and dance. Moving your body and using a song with real meaning has a profound effect. This is most effective in setting the tone for my day.

2. **Journalling (5–20 minutes).** Write down what is coming up for you or answer these questions:

   – What am I committed to creating today?

   – What am I letting go of today?

   – How do I want to feel at the end of today?

   – How can I be bolder than yesterday?

3. **Meditation (5–20 minutes).** I like to focus on visualising my day and intention setting. I also use affirmations and positive statements.

Your morning ritual will help you build that 'just do it' muscle and focus on doing what's important. There are also more practical tips in Chapter 6.

The answer hiding in plain sight

My morning ritual is key to keep me on track and get things done, but there is another way. What if I told you there is a way that you can guarantee you will make all of your goals and dreams come true, that there is a path for you to make things happen which doesn't involve willpower? Would you want to know what it is? Would you want to use that method every single time to ensure you always get things done?

Unfortunately, I'm pretty sure you won't like it.

There is one way that works for the Good Girl personality every single time and it's been hiding in plain sight all of your life. Ready?

External accountability – and not just any accountability either. Let's get into it.

When we first start a business we are at risk because no one knows what we're doing. There are no customers/

clients to start with and no one is checking up on our progress. In order to keep going, we need to pull on a serious amount of inner strength and intrinsic motivation. Many of us lose momentum at some point between the start and everything getting good; I know I have had business plans in the past that have fizzled out because I didn't have the impetus to go all in on them.

Parkinson's law states that work expands to fill the time we have to complete it.[29] This explains why our self-imposed deadlines don't work for us. We can move our own deadlines, so we don't have that last-minute energy that can be so motivating.

External accountability is an important tool that you can use to build momentum.

How many qualifications do you have?

I can almost guarantee that when you want to learn something new you are attracted to formal learning and certification programmes. There are many reasons for this, including:

- You know the curriculum has been curated for you, you don't have to search it out, find the right books to read and so on.

- You know there will be an expert to ask questions and gain clarity.

- You know there will be deadlines, and deadlines are like catnip for you. They help you stay on track because that external expectation helps you follow through to completion.

MY STORY: Four degrees

I have four degrees – two in psychology and two in education. I only did one full time; the rest I fit in while working full time. I say that not to brag but with a small amount of shame that I didn't cotton on to this after at least the second one. I was attracted to them to start with because the topics were interesting to me. I completed them because I had regular hard deadlines along the way to get the work done.

If you want to get something done, something you are intrinsically motivated to do, the absolute solid guaranteed way to ensure you will do it is to find a way to have external accountability for it. At this moment, I am writing this book at midnight because I have a month until my manuscript needs to be with my publisher. This external deadline means that I am prioritising getting it done now when I have a lot of other things to be doing too (like being asleep).

Not all external accountability works, though – why would it be that simple?

Getting things done

Let's look at ways that work for us and the things that don't.

Get a coach

I say this first because I am a business and mindset coach working one to one with my Good Girl Rebel clients, meeting with them online regularly to check in with them and their progress. I am a coach because I find it so rewarding to work one to one with people through their 'aha' moments and their milestones and to help mentor people with the shortcut strategies that will get there faster so they keep going.

I've had a few clients stay for a few months, stop and then come back because they realised the value of having that regular check in and subsequent progress on their business goals. When they didn't have it, they stalled out, even when they promised themselves faithfully they wouldn't.

I also employ coaches myself because it is my fast track to get to where I want to be in my business. I wouldn't recommend you hire me if I didn't believe and invest in coaching myself. A study from the ICF reported that 80% of those that received coaching reported an increase in self-confidence and 70% improved work performance.[30]

Join a group programme

Again, this is transparent because I run group programmes periodically throughout the year that are
designed to help the Good Girl get things done, but the
reason I run them is because they work for my clients
and research backs this up.[31,32]

If one-to-one coaching isn't the right thing for you,
being a part of a group can make a huge difference to
whether you get things done. There are three reasons
for this:

1. It is that date in your calendar where you need
   to say whether you've done what you said
   you would, which helps put a good amount of
   pressure on your goals.

2. It's about having a sounding board to ask
   questions, get unstuck quickly and keep moving.

3. Being a part of a group of women who all
   have big goals is motivating and can be
   mind-expanding.

Get an accountability partner

Accountability partners can be a great way to get
support and encouragement.[33] Not everyone makes
a good accountability partner. A friend and I tried to
be accountability partners for each other and it didn't

work. We'd talk on the phone once a month and promise faithfully to do things to grow our businesses. Lo and behold, four weeks would roll around and we had to share that we still had not done it. Your accountability partner needs to be someone who will hold you accountable and that you wouldn't want to let down.

Collaborate

Another thing that works well for us when managed right is collaborations and partnerships. When you're first starting a business, you have all the invisible architecture of the business to create before you can start selling to the customer/client, including a product/ service, website and socials. When it is all down to us we can struggle because there isn't any accountability. Until we get customers and consistent income, the Good Girls are at risk of giving up before it gets going and the profits come in.

Enter the business partnerships and collaborations. Finding ways to work with others is the secret to success. You may let yourself down, but you will never let anyone else down, so strategically setting up partnerships will help you feel more motivated and achieve more.

MY STORY: Easy collaboration

My *Full of Ourselves Podcast* has been the most natural and easy collaboration ever. Heidi Hinda Chadwick and I met when I was training as a life coach, doing my coaching hours for my ICF associate coach status. We gelled immediately and have been working together ever since. The podcast came from both our coaching conversations and a popular episode we recorded for a different podcast on comfort zones.

Working in collaboration has been a joy. We both have our parts to play, and because we respect each other it's easy to ensure that we meet our own deadlines. We bounce ideas off each other. If you've listened to the podcast (and if you haven't, I encourage you to!) you'll hear how well we align and work together.

Grow your network

'The Old Boys Network' is an English phrase particularly referring to upper-class men who went to boarding school and then know all the people in power. We can have our own network too by supporting and working with other women in collaboration. When someone needs an expert, you will know someone to recommend. This is important for us Good Girls and helps the world go round right. Networking is key to your success.

Announce it to the world

It's a bold strategy but tell people what is coming and when. If it's just your deadline you can move it, but if you've told everyone about it, there's that added pressure to make it happen.

Sell it before it exists

This is basically the same thing as announcing it to the world, and a lot of smart and rich business people suggest this strategy. Talk about your idea before you've made it and get pre-sales for your products/services. This allows you to test whether the idea will work before you invest your time and money in developing it. Once you've sold it, you know you need to deliver it and you'll be more motivated to do so because you already have the money in the bank. You've got customers waiting and the Good Girl will not let them down.

Apply for an award or show

I work a lot with product-based businesses. Getting your products in front of the right people can be a real game changer. This could be at a relevant trade show or other industry event. Often when you apply to these – especially the ones where spaces are coveted – you have to bring together lots of data for the judging panel. You will need to ensure you have your product range, branding and signage sorted. Applying for an award or getting into a show helps you get things done by a specific deadline.

Work in public

This is an interesting one that does work for some of us. When I first moved to Scotland, I rented a desk in a co-working space and I would go there to work every weekday. I often left my laptop there, so I had to get my work done while I was there. I also had lovely artists and creative business owners who were around to bounce ideas off and to check in with. This was pre-Covid and unfortunately that space no longer exists, but working in public – even in coffee shops – can help you stay on track. You can also try a virtual co-working space. These are set up with time limits and check ins so can be a good option.

Procrastinate

Maybe this is just me, but I find there is an optimum number of things that I have to get done and I can end up doing anything but the thing that is most urgent. I have no interest in cleaning, but when I have something urgent to do I can sometimes be found doing it. While I had just a few weeks left to submit my book, I created a whole merchandise range for the Good Girl Rebellion! For me this works because there is no way I won't meet the deadline so everything else that I get done along the way is a bonus. I'm not sure I can call this a strategy, but this sneaky way of distracting myself does get a lot of things done!

I can't 'just do it' – The paradox

I have been able to build my 'just do it' muscle through my morning ritual but I do acknowledge that the sure-fire easy way to ensure things happen is with external accountability. What I find interesting from reflecting on myself and the other Good Girl personalities that I've worked with over the years is a strange incon-sistency I've seen time and again. It's like the external deadline as a parameter is a relief. We don't have to second guess ourselves about what to do by when and we don't struggle to meet the deadline. It is different to not leaving things to the last minute. The energy of the last minute can be motivating to us, and maybe that is why self-imposed deadlines don't work: we can always move them so there is never that last-minute pressure to get us going.

When we try to force ourselves to do the things we really want to do, we rebel against it, but if we need to meet someone at a certain time we will. I wonder if the rules around working hours and deadlines in the workplace are just structure enough for us to work our magic within? If we try to get rigid with all aspects of our lives and set ourselves lots of rules, we just can't make ourselves do it, free will be damned.

Don't like this insistence on external accountability? I don't either and I resisted it for a long time. If that is how you're feeling, try the following exercise.

EXERCISE: Three in three

Write down three big goals you have for your business and break them down into the steps you need to take to get them done. Put an alert in your calendar three months from now to check in on your progress on those goals.

If you have made inroads into them without any external accountability, I take my hat off to you. You have more self-control, willpower and organisation than I ever will. If you see that notification in your calendar in three months' time and you have not made any significant movement towards those goals, find external accountability.

This is not some kind of failure. This is not me saying you don't have it in you. You have basically been programmed to prioritise everything and everybody else over yourself (see Chapter 2). What you need to do is to game that system and find the way to make this work for you, not against you.

Concluding from all the psychology I have read and shared about in this book, this works. What I want is for the Good Girl Rebels to win. Set yourself up right now to win.

Summary

- Good Girl personalities tend to struggle with intrinsic motivation, doing the things we want to do.

- 'Just do it' is not consistently motivating for us, although it is for some other personality types.

- Build your 'just do it' muscle with your own morning ritual.

- To get things done, Good Girls should: get a coach, join a group programme, get an accountability partner, collaborate, grow their network, announce it to the world, sell it before it exists, apply for an award or show, work in public and procrastinate.

- Finding ways to build in external accountability for the things you want to do is the secret to getting things done for the Good Girl Rebel.

Before we get to the REBEL methodology, let's have a look at what you're selling. Whether you have a product or service business (I've had both over the years), there are some important things to get clear on.

4

Your Offer

Before I get into the REBEL methodology, it's time to reflect on what you're selling, the vision you have for your business, the products/services to have and what the research shows most people will buy from you.

Your vision (and why it's OK if you don't have one)

Sometimes people have a clear vision of where they are going and sometimes they don't – either is OK. In my experience, people think that if they lack the big vision, it means that they're not on the right track and it can stop them from moving forwards.

Let's bust that myth. People see the world in different ways. Which do you most align with: goal-oriented or freedom-oriented?

MY STORY: The frog in hot water

Every job I've ever left is because I couldn't stand it anymore. I've had some toxic bosses whose demands and manner I could no longer stomach. I've been a full-time teacher measured by ridiculous benchmarks for things I couldn't control. I've been notified that my manager (one of the good ones) had dropped dead of a heart attack on the cricket pitch where he was umpiring a match for kids while we were preparing for Ofsted. That was the beginning of the end of my career in the formal teaching sector.

I am generally someone who stays too long in a situation and I end up leaving when I can't take it anymore and finally snap. This can be a pattern for us Good Girls – do you recognise that pattern in yourself too? We are often optimists, or at least realists.

It's like the story of the frog in hot water. If a frog is dropped into hot water, it will jump straight out; if it is put into the pot and the water heats up gently, it doesn't jump out. While this maxim may not actually be true of frogs (I've read that it's an urban myth), it's definitely been true for me. So many times, I've persevered somewhere that got increasingly difficult to stomach. When I finally got out of a situation and

---

looked back in hindsight, I wondered what I was thinking and how I stayed there.

There is a point to this that will help you understand how you're motivated. Some people are goal-oriented; others are freedom-oriented. Have a think about which you are as you read this next section.

Goal-oriented people have a goal that they are working on and a fairly clear vision of what that will look like. For some there is a big clear vision, but that isn't always the case and if you don't have that, don't worry. There's nothing wrong with you.

Other people are freedom-oriented (like me). They are more motivated by not doing or having things. 'I'm not living like this anymore,' 'I'm not working for that [insert appropriate swear word] anymore,' etc.

We can all be a bit of both, so take a look at the exercises below and do them all. Or if one side is calling to you more, do that one.

If you are goal-oriented

First, take a step back and ask yourself: 'What should I spend my time on?' There's no point in lots of busy-work that's not going to get you to where you want to go. The more specific you are about what you're aiming for, the more likely you are to be able to get there. Whether you have a clear vision of the outcome or you don't yet, here are three exercises to work through to help you get clarity.

EXERCISE 1: What are your wildest dreams, biggest goals, hugest hopes?

These goals can be around your work, home, family, health, relationships, friendships, hobbies – everything that's important for you. Start by posing the question to yourself and then take a walk, do something else and see what comes up. Keep writing down the dreams, goals and hopes that come to you until you have a good list that covers different areas of your life.

EXERCISE 2 : What would your ideal day look like?

Let's take it a step further. If you had everything on that list – if you'd achieved your biggest goals – what would your day look like? This should be a normal workday, not a holiday. Consider the following:

- Where are you?
- What do you do?
- What do you see?
- What does it feel like?
- What do you smell?

Spend some time thinking about this. Allow your mind to dream and engage all of your senses when imagining your ideal day.

EXERCISE 3: Reverse engineering your ideal life

It's time to work backwards so you can see how you can get there. What are the main themes that signal success to you? Is it having a seven-figure business, a team that works for you, a beautiful house or a great relationship? Pick out the main areas that you need to work on to achieve your ideal life.

For example, if I want to build my coaching business, I need to devote time every day to working on my content creation and brand development.

I want to be healthy and active in old age so I need to start that now. I look at what I eat, focus on walking and exercise, etc.

You are the CEO of your life and your business. Dedicating time to setting clear goals will help you use your time effectively in the pursuit of yourself – not just your business.

It's easy to stay busy doing small things and not look up at what will make the biggest impact. Take the time to do this exercise and work on these important areas and one day that ideal day will be today.

If you are freedom-oriented

If you are more freedom-oriented or you don't have a big vision for what you want, give this exercise a try.

EXERCISE: The 'I don't want to' list

Start a page in your journal and write down the things you no longer want to tolerate in your life. Leave a few pages blank and let your unconscious mind work on the task too, writing ideas down as they come to you over the next few days. These can be as petty as you like. Here are some prompts and ideas that I came up with:

- I don't want to work with...
- I don't want to spend my time on...
- I don't want to feel...
- I don't want to be around...

Let this percolate for a week or so before the next step, as it will then have more value.

Once you have your 'I don't want' list, write out the opposite. For example:

- 'I don't want to work with people who manipulate me, who aren't interested in me and my wellbeing' *becomes* 'I want to work with people who value me, who care about and are invested in my wellbeing and who I love being around'.
- 'I don't want to work full time' *becomes* 'I want to work flexibly and look forward to my work'.

This will frame your goals in a positive mindset, making you realise what you truly value.

The products/services you need in your business

Whether you are selling products or services, research shows that it is important to have things available at three different price points. This helps guide people about what to buy from you.

The three price points are:

1. A no-brainer offer – something worth £50/$50 or under

2. Your signature offer – what most people will buy from you at an average price

3. A high-ticket item

This doesn't mean you only sell three things (although that may be the case for some people). You could have a few products at the lower price point, one signature offer and one or more high-ticket offers. I haven't put prices on all of these because it does depend on your product/service and the average sales figures (and we'll get into pricing in detail in Chapter 8).

What do most people buy? The middle-priced item. Some will buy the no-brainer offer first and then move up. A few people will know they want your high-ticket item so it's good to have this option available, but the vast majority of people will buy your signature offer and that's what you want to become known for.

The psychology of choice

The reason for having three price points or brackets is clear from the research. Simonson and Tversky conducted a study where they offered people a choice between two cameras and found that around half the group chose one and half chose the other. When they did the same experiment with three cameras, the majority chose the middle option.[34] This is borne out by other experiments, including one by Starbucks, who have always found that people choose the middle option. When Starbucks removed the smallest coffee size and added an even larger one, 'the Venti', people tended to choose the middle option even when their original size choice was still on the menu.[35]

We also want there to be choice, but not too much. Schwartz found that too much choice can actually make people anxious and lead to decision fatigue, and if people do choose they start to wonder if they've made the right decision.[36]

In a study about jam by Iyengar and Lepper that I love, researchers experimented by putting out two tables in a supermarket. One had six jams that people could try and the other had twenty-four jams for people to try.

While more people stopped to try when there were more samples, there were ten times more sales when there were just six jams to choose between.[37]

What does this mean for you? It is worth reviewing what you currently sell, or if you're just starting out, factor this into your plans.

What to do if you're not making any money

First, let me reiterate that it can take a few years for a business to start making a profit and building your momentum is important.[38] We'll talk more about this in Chapter 7.

For now, if you want to make money, you need to have something out in the world that people can purchase. It sounds obvious but sometimes people can get to the end of a launch (how to launch is also coming up in Chapter 7) and find that they don't have the next one lined up so their income dips. The answer is to ensure you have a revenue-generating activity each quarter.

A revenue-generating activity is anything you are going to be particularly promoting. You may be going all out, for example for product-based businesses, Christmas can be a big opportunity and if your work is giftable you may make up to 70% of your annual income at this time. If you are a coach, then the beginning of the year can be a great opportunity to talk about how you can help and support people.

The key is to plan them in advance for the year. If that feels too much, at least know what your plan is for the next quarter, so you know what is coming up and you don't have any blank spaces.

Your first launches may not make money. That is the brutal truth but knowing it now means that you can keep going. It's not that what you are doing or selling is wrong. You may need to tweak things, but when we start to sell we are teaching our customers/clients what we have and what we do. Persistence is the key.

EXERCISE: Plan your revenue-generating activities

Get a piece of paper and draw a line down the centre and across the middle. You should have four sections, which we'll use to represent the next four quarters. The quarters are January to March, April to June, July to September and October to December.

If you are just at the start of a quarter, make that the first box at the top left. If you are close to the end of a quarter, start your planning with the next one.

Plan out your revenue-generating activities for each of the next four quarters. This should just be an overall plan; it's not about the detail at this stage. Reflecting on what you are going to sell – whether it's something new or sharing about something

---

that you already have – is an important part of your strategy.

We'll come back to this exercise in Chapters 6 and 7.

Summary

- Knowing whether you are goal-oriented or freedom-oriented can help you when you are crafting your vision for your business.

- Design an offer with three price points: a no-brainer, a signature offer and a high-ticket offer.

- Choice is good but not too much!

- Plan your promotions and launches for the next quarter at least, ensuring you have something for people to purchase at all times.

PART TWO
THE REBEL
METHODOLOGY

When I realised that all of the methods I'd been faith-fully trying to use just didn't work for me, I tore it all up and made my own. The REBEL methodology is a game changer.

REBEL is a handy acronym that stands for:

- **R**esilient mindset – How we see our world *is* our world. All business issues are mindset issues, so let's clear away our fears and blocks to success.

- **E**veryday action – We need to find the right ways to make progress on our business every workday. Why do the time management strategies that others love give you the 'ick'? What do you do instead?

- **B**old marketing – We need to be our own champions. That is not always a natural space for the Good Girl, so let's work out how we can do it.

- Empowered pricing – You have a lot to offer and you deserve to make a good living from what you do, so let's clear the money blocks and look at how to price correctly.

- Liberating results – When we do everything that comes before, the results will follow and that's when everything changes.

In this part of the book we will look at each tenet of the REBEL methodology in more detail, so we can each begin our own Good Girl Rebellion.

5

Resilient Mindset

It is no coincidence that the first tenet of the REBEL methodology is resilient mindset. Your mindset is not just important, it's fundamental to who you are and how you act. When we think about growing a business, we're likely focusing on testing that our product or service is viable, learning how to build a website and how to market – we will get to all of that in this book. Your mindset may not be your priority when growing a business, but it is what will make or break both your business and you having a happy life. In this chapter, we're going to look at what we do with fear, imposter syndrome and self-sabotage.

I first chose to study psychology at university because I was fascinated by perception, and I still am thirty years later. I saw in the people around me that how we see our world *is* our world. Our thoughts become things and our actions are a consequence of our thoughts. The research bears this out. The exact same day can feel very different depending on what we look for.

MY STORY: Focus on the positive

Recently, my husband and I took a break away. The company we had booked our holiday with rang a few days before to say that our cabin had been damaged in a storm and we could no longer stay there. Fortunately, we were able to find somewhere else to stay that was a couple of hours further away. We don't have a car so we went to the car hire place to pick one up. We parked outside our building and started to pack up the car. Just as we were about to leave, we noticed we had a parking ticket! We have a resident permit but had forgotten to put one in the window in our haste to get moving. It was a bad start to our break and the weather on the way up to the Highlands wasn't great either. It was very wet, so we had to take the journey slowly.

It would have been easy to allow these things to taint the start of our holiday, but luckily we didn't. We focused on the fact that we could get away. We got in the hot tub and laughed at the rain. In the end, the weather in the new location was pretty good with clear skies for stargazing at night from the hot tub, which is my favourite thing to do. I emailed the building management about the parking ticket and hoped they could help ensure our stupidity wasn't punished.

This is not a story of hardship – we are fortunate and that is my point. Whatever we have we can focus on the negative and all the things going wrong or we can focus on the positive. Whatever we focus on grows in our minds.

If you're thinking to yourself, 'Oh no. I'm not an optimist, I'm a realist on a good day and a pessimist the rest of the time. What hope is there for me?' Don't worry. There is a lot we can do to improve our mindset, and this chapter gives you some concrete ways to do that.

All business issues are mindset issues

When it comes down to it, all issues, including around your business, are mindset issues. Don't believe me? Let's get into a few examples:

- You work on a product or service and delay releasing it to the world because there always seems to be something more that needs to be done before it's ready – the copy needs tweaking, new photos need to be taken or you need to get your branding finished.

- You know you need to promote your business but you feel inhibited. You don't want people to be bored with your business, you struggle with being visible and you fear being criticised and called out for what you do.

- You find out you are qualified to apply for an industry award but don't apply because imposter syndrome kicks in and you think you'll be 'found out', then the person who wins is less experienced and less qualified than you.

- You're invited to speak about your business at a big networking event. This event has lots of your ideal customers and clients and is a brilliant opportunity for you to showcase how you can work with them. Your fear of public speaking means you decline because you just can't face it.

- You have the opportunity to work with someone you admire and don't because you just don't feel worthy.

The root of all these decisions is one thing: fear. That fear can be holding you back.

You are standing in your own way

Your fear is manipulative, affecting what you think is possible and how you act in the world. To understand this we need to understand how the mind works. There are plenty of great books that go deep into the science (see the Endnotes); for now, know the following:

Researchers have concluded that our brains have evolved to focus more on the negative than the positive.[39] I'm sure you've already worked this out for yourself. If you get 100 positive comments on a social media post and two negative comments – what will you focus on? The negative is going to outweigh the positive and weigh on your mind. You might be tempted to chastise yourself for that, but this happens for a reason.

Your beautiful brain evolved to keep you safe. It was better for your survival to know to avoid the bushes with poisonous berries than to know which held the delicious berries. Fortunately for us, our day-to-day survival (at least in most of the Western world) no longer hinges on us being able to avoid the negative, but evolution is a slow process and our brain hasn't got the memo. Our thriving, in life and business, depends on our ability to override this natural fear response to focus more on our goals than our fears. It's no wonder that so many businesses fail when the same mind that creates your goals is the one creating the stories that are holding you back. If you know about this, you can do something about it.

EXERCISE: Let's play fear bingo

How many of these fears have you felt in your life and business:

- Failure
- Success
- Public speaking
- Financial insecurity
- Judgement
- Rejection

- Not being perfect
- People won't come to my event
- People won't buy from me
- I'm wasting my time
- I'm wasting my money
- Burnout
- Making the wrong decision
- Self-promotion
- Being too much or not enough

Do you have a full house?

If you have a full house or have had many of these fears, all that means is that you're human. It does not mean you're not worthy of all that you dream of or you're not capable of achieving those dreams. Bravery isn't a lack of fear, it's acting despite the fear. How do we do that? Let's get into it.

Fight, flight or freeze?

The evolutionary explanation for stress and fear is that when we perceive a threat we go into fight, flight or freeze mode in order to keep ourselves safe. While we can do all three, we tend towards one of these. As you read the following examples, think which most closely resembles how you respond when stressed about your business.

If you tend towards 'fight' you are likely to become more assertive, possibly even aggressive, in the face of challenges. This can lead to being confrontational to try to clear the air. You can become over-controlling and a perfectionist when it comes to your business and find it difficult to accept support and help.

'Flight' is all about avoidance and escape from the issues. That can manifest as procrastination and withdrawing from the thing you know you need to address while using distraction tactics that numb you.

'Freeze' is where you shut down. This can lead to a struggle to make decisions. You can end up feeling stuck, indecisive and avoid confrontation, even when you know you need to deal with the issue.

On the whole, Good Girls tend towards flight or freeze. This can end up delaying your progress and, in the extreme, result in you giving up.

Now we know what we're up against, how do we deal with fear?

How we deal with fear

It may feel like a hopeless task to try to override the way your brain works but it's not. Research shows that we can make changes to our thinking.[40] You need to find a way to step outside of your thoughts and notice your brain's regular programming to move out of fear and survival into growth. Here is how.

Step 1: Notice your thoughts

The first step to success is to notice your thoughts. One of my absolute favourite quotes is: 'You are not your thoughts, you are the thinker of your thoughts.' This means your thoughts may not be true. We can get stuck on 'automatic thoughts' – those stories you have about why you can't do and can't have something. We can change these through learning, habit and repetitive thinking.[41]

Step 2: Get curious

It's time to make friends with your fear. Sounds easy and fun, right? What you need to realise is that your fear response, whether it is out of proportion or not, is there to keep you safe, and that is a good thing. If you can start thinking of your fear as a cautious friend trying to keep you from doing anything stupid, you can begin to understand it. That doesn't mean you have to do what it says, but it does mean you can look on your fear with understanding and gratitude for all it tries to do for you.

Courage, competence, confidence – unfortunately, it does have to go in that order. We are often waiting for confidence before we get started, but bravery is not the absence of fear. The only way out of fear is to act, so you need to get curious about what the fear is trying to protect you from. Ask it: 'What are you trying to protect me from? What are you afraid of?'

When we try to deny and push down our fears, they just come back stronger. It's like when a friend warns you about something but you start to do it anyway and the friend starts shouting because they don't think you are taking their warning seriously.

Listen to what your fear is telling you and ask one question: 'Is it true?' This profound question from Byron Katie's *The Work* helps you stop being stuck in fear and start questioning it.[42] When we question our thoughts, we step away from the fear and start to analyse it. In doing so, we are no longer quite as gripped by our body's fear response of fight, flight or freeze.

Step 3: Take action

It can be tempting to spend time analysing yourself, but if you keep all your focus on asking, 'Why am I feeling this way?', you will only stay in that feeling because that is what you are obsessing over. To move through it, ask yourself two important questions:

1. What do I need right now?

2. What would I do right now if I really loved myself?

When you have some compassion for yourself and your fear, you will feel a shift – a tiny bit of space that leaves you open to start moving in the right direction. Doing one thing – it could be a big bold move or a tiny step in the right direction – is key. To not get stuck in flight or freeze, we need to take meaningful action.

Imposter syndrome

One of the big places where we see our fear in action is with imposter syndrome. This is when you feel like a fraud and that you'll be found out at any moment. It happens any time you are trying to make changes to your life, so if you're feeling imposter syndrome, congratulations; you want something more from your life.

Imposter syndrome is fundamentally about an identity shift – we are used to having one identity and suddenly we are trying to create a new one.

The same advice on questioning your fear applies here but I also think it is helpful to remember that every expert was once a beginner. More than ever with social media we are seeing those with self-proclaimed expertise around us and we feel like we're falling short, but that is false. Don't fear failure, fear being in the same place a year from now.

Self-sabotage

Self-sabotage is the last-ditch attempt of fear. It is where we consciously or unconsciously think or behave in a way that inhibits our success. If you spot self-sabotage patterns showing up, get excited because you are close to a breakthrough and your fear can't stand it.

Fear is usually shouty and judgemental. It says things like, 'What do you think you're doing? Who do you think you are? This is too risky; it's time to stop.' If the shouting doesn't work to stop you, fear starts to get sneaky and fear manifests as self-sabotage.

The three stages of self-sabotage

Our self-sabotage patterns have our own unique flavour and blend. I was speaking with my friend and coach Heidi Hinda Chadwick about this and she said something that made me pause. She said, 'People tend to struggle with either the beginning, middle or end of a project.' As you read the following, reflect on where self-sabotage comes up for you.

If you struggle at the beginning of a project, you likely struggle with the overwhelm of getting started. You may be a perfectionist. Perhaps you have many beautiful pristine notebooks that you have yet to write in because you don't want to mess them up.

If you struggle in the middle of a project, you can capitalise on the energy you feel at the start but then you find it difficult to stay motivated. Suddenly a new idea seems infinitely more exciting than carrying out an idea that's lost its sparkle.

If you struggle at the end of the project, you have a fear of failure or a fear of success. After all this work you've put in, what if it doesn't work out? What if you've given it your all and it's not enough? Or what if it does all work out and you get inundated?

EXERCISE: Self-sabotage – where do you get off track?

Once you've identified your self-sabotage pattern, get your journal out and ask these questions:

- **What am I afraid will happen if I continue?** This question helps you identify the specific fear that is holding you back.

- **What story am I telling myself in this moment?** This question helps you reflect on where you need to work on the narrative in your head. For example, are you telling yourself that you're not ready, that you're going to mess it up, that people won't care, that no one will buy?

- **What support would be helpful right now?** When self-sabotage comes up we can feel stuck. This question helps you move through that to how things can move forward. It could be that you need to rest, to assert your boundaries, to keep going and ignore the fears, etc.

This is a powerful exercise that will allow you to spot the self-sabotage pattern coming up and help you interrupt it in the future.

Spotting your patterns and where self-sabotage comes up for you is helpful because you can be ready for it. This is not a battle with fear but a real understanding and appreciation of where it is trying to help you.

Here are some common self-sabotage patterns – perfectionism and procrastination – and what to do if you spot them.

Perfectionism

The perfectionist in business wants everything to be just right before they release to the world, yet what often happens is you keep moving the goalposts. When one thing is dealt with suddenly something else comes up that absolutely has to be sorted out before the product can be launched, the pitch can be made, etc.

The antidote to perfectionism? Remembering that success depends on high standards and not being flawless. Flawless isn't interesting and we don't want perfection, we want excellence. We may not get there immediately, but if we keep working, we'll get there. This is all a part of the experience, not a destination.

Procrastination

Delaying making a decision or following through on an action because of overwhelm or indecision can be a real struggle for Good Girl personalities.

The antidote to procrastination? If it's getting the task done, go back to Chapter 3 which is all about how we move through that. If you delay because you struggle to make decisions, you're not alone. There is more on decision-making in the next chapter.

The transformational power of gratitude

The antidote to fear is gratitude. When we can be grateful for what we have while working towards growing and wanting more, we can have happiness.

Gratitude is a skill you can practise, and it is essential to your success that you do. As I mentioned at the beginning of the chapter, how we see our world *is* our world – perception is key. The negative part of our brain and judgement naturally overrides the positive part, but fortunately you can change your perception and become a more positive thinker by practising gratitude.

Here are some concrete ways to do this:

- **End of the day**: At the end of your day, when brushing your teeth, think of three things from your day that you are grateful for. Pairing this with a task you do automatically helps ensure you remember to do it.

- **Gratitude journalling**: If you struggle with your mental health and negative thinking, I get it. I suggest starting a gratitude journal. Every night, write down five things you are grateful for from your day. They can be small things like a smile from a stranger or getting to the bus stop just in time to catch the bus, big things like achievements from your day or anything in between. Write these down each day and take the time to be grateful in the moment.

- **'Everything works out for me' notebook**: This has been a game changer for me. I have a notebook that is just for this purpose (what can I say, I am a stationery addict!). At the end of most days, I write down when things have worked out for me.

- **Write a 'ta-da' list**: This is a fantastic suggestion from Gretchen Rubin. I have a 'ta-da' list at the back of my journal that I use to write down things that happen that I feel proud of, such as a great email I receive, finishing a project, selling out an event, etc. When I read it back, I've often forgotten some of the things on it in my rush to keep moving forwards. It's a great way to record your achievements and something to look at when you are feeling overwhelmed.

Summary

- Your mindset is fundamental to who you are and how you act. There is a lot we can do to improve our mindset.

- All business issues are mindset issues.

- Our fear is the biggest obstacle to having the growth and success that we want.

- We deal with fear by remembering that it is there to try to keep us safe. We can listen to what it has to say and still do what we want to do.

- Good Girls tend towards flight or freeze, rather than fight.

- To deal with fear, notice your thoughts, get curious then take action.

- Self-sabotage happens just as we're about to succeed. It is the last attempt from fear to stop us.

- Imposter syndrome, perfectionism and procrastination are all fear in different guises.

- The antidote to fear is gratitude. Getting into the habit of being grateful helps shift our focus onto the positive in life.

The next chapter looks at the second tenet of the REBEL methodology: everyday action – the practical actions you can take each day to make decisions and get things done.

6
Everyday Action

If I am honest with myself, I'd like to get results in my business without any risk, without it being hard and without it taking lots of emotional, physical and financial investment. Basically, I want the results without the work. What about you?

You and I both know that this is delusional.

Let's take a step back. Would you want someone else to have everything you have right now without the work you've put in and the experiences you've had?

Let's look at those who have had that unicorn experience. The child actors making it big before they have the skills to deal with it. The teenage prodigy musicians and footballers who can't cope with the fame. The lottery winners who no longer know who their friends are.

Building a successful business can take time and effort. It can take a few years to start making a profit.[43] I don't say that to put you off, I say it to encourage you to take the longer view. You can and will get there if you keep going, adjust your direction when you need to and find a way to get the work done every day. That's what this chapter is all about.

The second tenet of the REBEL methodology is every-day action. It is the simple truth that building a business takes time and consistent effort. Working on it every workday sounds obvious but it's not easy, particularly for Good Girl personalities, so if you have struggled with this in the past, be kind to yourself.

In this chapter, we're going to talk decision-making. I'm going to tell you why you struggle with day-to-day actions and why a lot of time management strategies give you the 'ick'. I'll give you some strategies that work well for us Good Girl Rebels for you to try. Chapter 3 has also helped with this as it addressed the wider issues of getting things done. Here we focus on the practical things you can do each day to get the work done and build momentum.

Decision-making

Decision-making is part of our job description as business owners, yet it can be challenging for the Good Girl. There are several reasons for this. One is a consequence of our empathy. We are excellent at anticipating what everyone needs and that bigger-picture thinking can lead to overwhelm. You likely can see the consequences of your decisions playing out in your mind and that makes deciding which way to go more challenging. Also, if you've spent your career working for someone else, you haven't been the one making final decisions on big goals, perhaps ones on investing large sums or saying no to opportunities. Even with experience as a senior manager in a business, I have found having the decision-making power all to myself intimidating at times.

Tips for Good Girls on making decisions

If a decision is easy, it's not a decision. By that I mean that if one solution is obvious to you, you don't have to think about it, you just do that. If you're stuck with a decision, it's because there isn't an easy answer. I find that a comforting thought.

In the book *Feel the Fear and Do It Anyway*, Susan Jeffers talks about the choice point. We come to a place where we need to make a decision and we imagine that one decision is going to be the right one with only good consequences and the other will be the wrong one with only negative consequences.[44] Jeffers astutely argues that is not true. There are good and bad things about any decision we make and if we get stuck thinking we've made the wrong choice, we can end up second guessing ourselves and doubting.

I have been fortunate to work for successful entrepreneur Jessica Rose. She has founded multiple successful businesses, and I have seen first-hand her day-to-day decision-making when growing three different businesses. One thing that always struck me is her sense of urgency. She consults on her decisions and then, once a decision is made, she'll set timelines and deadlines and work towards those. She doesn't waver on it and keeps moving forwards.

One of the most important beliefs I hold is that I always make the best decision I can with the information I have available. With hindsight, it may turn out not to be the right decision, but I need to not get too judgy over my past self.

Managing your time

If you are starting your business alongside other commitments like a job, it's time to get strategic. I suggest having workdays for your business. They may not be the same days every week, but knowing which days you'll be working is important.

A lot of the traditional advice on time management gives me the 'ick' and I will happily throw the time management books I've read out the window. When I think about it in terms of being a bold and brilliant businesswoman, I get why it's important.

Plan for your week

I am not an advocate of time blocking and my calendar looking chock full of obligations. It makes me feel suffocated and is much more likely to have me cowering under a blanket than smashing my goals.

Just to be clear, what I mean by time blocking is filling your calendar with your to-do list on an hour-by-hour basis. If time blocking works for you – fantastic, go for it. If you're like me and it feels too much, here is what to do.

Plan at the end of your week

Before I finish my working week, I spend ten minutes looking at my commitments for the following week and work out when I will spend time on my business. Even if I just have thirty minutes for work on a particular day, I will have in mind that I will do something.

I then work out the tasks I have to fit the time available. If I've got a whole day available for work then great, I'll look at scheduling a bigger task. If I've got a small amount of time, I'll plan accordingly.

The 'future me' list

One of the biggest mistakes we make is the to-do list. It never ends and we don't get to feel a sense of accomplishment. I need a list of tasks, but I call it my 'future me' list – maybe it is a to-do list with another name, but I find it less demoralising! There is, of course, always something else to do and that can mean I don't give myself the credit for my achievements because I have low level anxiety about what's not done. For some reason, the 'future me' list works better because it's not taunting me with all the things I haven't done today.

One task a day – not a whole list

Full credit to Jessica Rose for this idea, which has really helped me. I plan in advance one thing that I want to achieve tomorrow and then do that. If I can get more done, great, but the plan is to do that one thing. It's so easy to end up doing a lot but the list is still there taunting me with all I haven't managed to achieve. Let's ditch the tyranny of the to-do list!

Avoid multitasking and context switching

Multitasking is OK when one of the tasks is automatic, for example walking and listening to a podcast, but when it comes to tasks that need some brain power we can struggle to focus on more than one thing. It can take up to twenty minutes to get our focus back when we're interrupted.[45]

Content batching can work well – doing similar tasks together, which saves on context switching. When we need to switch between types of tasks it takes more cognitive stress than when we do similar tasks together. Get strategic and batch tasks that are similar together; for example, plan to write and schedule all your emails for the month in one day. By bringing types of tasks together, we help ourselves and our concentration levels.

Eat that frog or start gently?

You may have seen the book, *Eat That Frog!*, which basically means do the worst thing first, get it out of the way and then you can enjoy the day.[46] I find that when I sit down to work, I often need to ease myself in gently! Starting with an easy part of my one thing to do today can be helpful and start building momentum for me. As with everything, it's about reflecting on what will work best for you and doing that.

When do you have the most energy?

Knowing when you have the best energy levels and concentration is important. There's no point in planning to do something that requires concentration after lunch if you know that is a real slump time for you because you're setting yourself up to fail and feel bad.

Many people argue for getting straight to work in the mornings but others prefer to work in the evenings (as I am right now as I write).

I've always been fascinated about the routines of creatives and in reading all about them, I learnt something surprising. Anything works as long as it works for you. Some people work early in the morning and others work late at night. Some work from their beds, others need to go to an office. There are infinite variations on what works.

If you already know the patterns that work best for you then great. If not, decide now to notice those ebbs and flows of your energy, motivation and focus.

Boundaries

I was walking along, getting ready to cross a side street and I looked at the cars passing by, keeping an eye out for anyone indicating to turn into the road I was about to cross. No car had their indicators on so I started to cross the road and just as I did, the car nearest to me turned into the road. I hate it when people don't indicate. Are you guilty of doing just that yourself in your business? I know I have been.

As I mentioned earlier, every job I've ever left has been because I was done with it; my boundaries were stomped on. As a Good Girl, I can acknowledge that I did not enforce my own boundaries, and actually that's not just detrimental to me, that isn't good for anyone. I have to acknowledge that the people I worked with thought that how they treated me was OK because I didn't tell them otherwise. If we have expectations but don't communicate them, those expectations are actually secrets. When I finally rebelled, it tended to be in a big drama of resignation and burnt bridges rather than being dealt with way before it got to that point with a calm enforcement of my boundaries. Sound familiar?

If you tend towards being a people pleaser – and many Good Girls are recovering people pleasers – you need to know that you can be difficult to work with. You can say yes to something and be resentful about it, which can impact your working relationships. This took me a long time and lots of painful encounters to embody. Our high empathy means that we can feel more for the other person than we do for ourselves. We can say yes to things we need to say no to because we like being needed and we are pleased we were asked. Today is the right time to draw a line under this behaviour for the good of yourself but also of those you are doing business with.

How do I say no?

Here is the magic phrase to say every time someone asks you to do something: 'Thank you for thinking of me. I have some commitments I'm working on right now so I'll check what I can do and get back to you.'

In the moment you might want to say yes, then later on you feel resentful and overworked. This one phrase is not a no, but it is a way of getting breathing space so you bypass your inner people pleaser and can make a decision from your rational brain based on whether you actually have the time.

What is a boundary?

A boundary is a clearly defined limit that you establish to protect your time, energy values and resources.

How do you know where you need boundaries? Some boundaries are quite obvious and clear cut and these are easier to deal with. For example, here are some business boundaries to communicate:

- Product/service descriptions

- Lead times

- How much access people have to you and the time you are available

You should be as clear as possible, so that no one is under any doubt about what you are able to do for them. Communicate this in:

- Product/service descriptions
- Frequently asked questions (FAQs) on your website
- Your out-of-office message
- Your email signature
- Clear policies
- Contracts

Other boundaries are a little harder to identify and come up as we move through the world. You will have boundaries that you don't know about yet so when someone has stepped over an invisible line, notice that it's happened and get curious. What about this situation has stepped over a boundary? Is it the task they've asked me to do? Is it the time I have to do it? Is it that it is expected of me and I wasn't asked? There could be lots happening and it's worth spending some time working out the cause of the issue for you so you can ensure that you pre-empt it from happening in the future.

What to do when a boundary is overstepped

If it's a business boundary, assume that they haven't read your policies and be clear about them, then ensure that your policies are clear – sharpen them up if there is some misunderstanding. If it is something else, it's worth taking some time out before responding to the person to allow the emotion you are feeling to subside.

You need to address it clearly. I personally like to do this in writing because it can save issues of miscommunication and being interrupted. You can ensure you are clear with your message and read it over before sending. That's not always possible, of course, so writing out what you are feeling before talking to the person is also a good strategy.

How to enforce boundaries

If this is something you know you need to work on, I recommend *The Book of Boundaries* by Melissa Urban,[47] in which she gives great examples of how to deal with boundaries. One great perspective I learnt from Melissa is that boundaries are about what *you* will do, not what the other person will do. Enforcing boundaries is not about controlling someone else, so you share the consequence of overstepping the boundary, e.g. if you bring this up again then I will do X. You must follow through on it, so don't set a consequence you know you will find difficult to enforce.

Here are some examples:

- If you've said you won't reply to emails outside of office hours don't, even if a message is urgent. People learn how to treat you from what you do, not just what you say. Even better, don't look at your messages out of office hours!

- If you have agreed to a certain scope of work, ensure that the task doesn't creep outside of those boundaries.

- Set a maximum number of client meetings you will have in a day or events you will do in a month to help avoid burnout.

EXERCISE: Designing your day

It's journalling time! I encourage you to reflect on a few areas that have come up in this chapter:

- When do you feel most focused and energised in your day?

- How can you protect that time of day to focus on your work?

- What activities for your business can you batch together to capitalise on your attention and focus?

- What boundaries can you set – for yourself and for others – to help you protect your time and your mental space?

- What one thing can you do today to build your business?

Getting this right will help you turbo-charge
your progress. These questions are worth asking
yourself every quarter to see if you have any deeper
reflections.

Productivity and seasons

We have forgotten the importance of the seasons, and
I mean that for ourselves and for our businesses. The
Industrial Revolution and invention of the lightbulb
meant that we were no longer held back needing to
work in the hours of daylight. The factory model of
working is, by its very nature, all about productivity.
It's 'go, go, go' all of the time. We don't have to work
like that. If we try to, that is the recipe for burnout.

In a Western capitalist society, it is an act of rebellion to
honour our own rhythms and patterns. I suspect that
part of your motivation for starting your business is to
have complete control over your time and location. You
don't have to work full time. Or you can choose to for
some of the time and then take proper time out. Really,
whatever pattern you want is what you should have.

MY STORY: Flexibility in my work

Here in the northern hemisphere right now it is
winter. I got up early because I have an external
deadline for my book, and I am starting to feel

the pressure! It's cold and I have a heated blanket draped over me right up to my armpits. The light in my room is on because, while there is daylight, it's not bright enough to work by. I feel fortunate to live in a country that has marked seasons (although many of us in Scotland grumble about a lack of a good summer!). The snowdrops are just starting to come through, spring will be here before I know it (as will my book deadline).

Another reason I got up early is that my husband and I are going to play pool this morning. It's Wednesday and I love that we both have the flexibility with work that we can just take a morning out and do what we want. For me, that is the real freedom of working for myself and building a business I love; that is the definition of success.

At the moment, I prefer to run shorter group programmes rather than have an annual membership. That may change by the time you are reading this, of course! I also tend to schedule all my one-to-one coaching sessions in two or three weeks in the month (depending on the number of clients I have) and have a week without obligations. This allows me to travel if I want, which brings a feeling of freedom and expansiveness. I like to have space in my calendar; it's probably back to the 'ick' I have around time blocking and feeling too controlled.

Have seasons in your business – it is like growing vegetables. There is a time for sowing seeds where we are busy getting out there and reaching a new audience. There is a time where we are harvesting, making sales and providing the products and services we have promised. There also needs to be a fallow time. A fallow field is one that is left without growing for a period of time to regenerate the soil and the nutrients. Farmers know that if they kept on farming the same land over and over again, it eventually gets depleted. We are the same. We need to build in time for rest. If your business has grown to a size where you find this difficult, it is past time to employ staff who can manage the day to day so you can rest.

Summary

- Building a profitable business takes time and consistency. If you keep moving forwards and taking your everyday action you will get there.

- Decision-making can be challenging for Good Girl personalities.

- Get strategic with managing your time. At the end of each week, look at the week ahead and the time you have for your business and plan to achieve one thing per workday.

- Keep a 'future me' list rather than a to-do list, and avoid multitasking – batch types of tasks together, e.g. writing emails for the month. Work when you know you have the most energy.

- Boundaries are about what *you* will do, not about controlling the other person. Set up your policies and descriptions to ensure your boundaries are maintained.

- Enforce your boundaries by concluding that people don't realise they are stepping over them and reminding them what they are.

- Productivity can be seasonal. You need a fallow time to recharge.

The third tenet of our REBEL methodology is bold marketing – getting your message out there – which we will explore in the next chapter.

7
Bold Marketing

Unfortunately, it is not a case of 'if you build it they will come'. At every stage of your business growth – but particularly at the beginning – bold marketing is key to your success. This chapter is all about how you can do just that.

As the speaking coach Dani Wallace so eloquently puts it, 'Closed mouths don't get fed.'[48] Potential customers and clients need to know about your business and what you do, and you're the person who needs to get the word out.

Good Girls can struggle with self-promotion. It stands to reason that we were more often the quiet ones at the back of the class, getting on with our work (and likely getting away with much more than people realised) rather than seeking attention. We need to find our way to get the message out. In this chapter we're going to look at you, your message and the way you get that out in the world. This could be a whole book in itself, so this chapter is a whistlestop tour through some of the key themes that come up for us when it comes to marketing.

MY STORY: A self-fulfilling failure

I had a big launch flop and what I learnt from it goes all the way back to the fear I was talking about in Chapter 4. It felt like I'd been building up to this launch for months. I'd had a successful smaller programme before it and I was hoping to build on that success, then the fear took over. What if no one buys? What if I've put everything into this and it fails? I was sure I'd feel devastated.

I took my foot off the gas and I didn't go all in with my marketing. I thought if I wasn't all in then any failure could be put down to that and not that it wasn't good enough or people didn't care. Surprise, surprise, I didn't make enough sales and the programme couldn't run. My self-fulfilling prophecy came to pass.

It is, of course, true that if I had gone all in and I'd still not made the sales I'd be in the same position I landed in, at least financially. My fear perhaps saved my self-esteem, but it didn't move my business forward.

Locus of control

As I talk about this, have a think about where your locus of control is for your business.

Locus of control refers to the extent to which you believe you have control over the events in your life and business.[49] If you have an internal locus of control, you act from a general belief that you are in control of what happens in your life. If you have an external locus of control, you believe that external forces are at play in what happens, including the economy, luck and others around you.

The Good Girl personality tends to be self-sufficient – often stubbornly and excessively so – and hold the belief that we get back what we put into life. As such, we are more likely to hold an internal locus of control, but this can go the other way and mean that when we do have setbacks, we take all of the blame on ourselves and conclude that we don't have what it takes and that our product/service won't succeed. More recent research suggests that the balance is tipping, and that people are generally becoming more externally focused than before.[50] I have seen this recently with coaching clients. Both the news and the economy can be scary, and that fear can end up inhibiting us from getting our business out there. There will always be people with money ready to spend it, so focusing on yourself and your customers is the best way forward.

It is likely that a healthy balance of both internal and external locus of control is important. You need to be bold and put in the effort to promote your business while knowing that external factors may come into play. The first few launches you do may not make the money that you want to make and will likely centre on educating your audience about what you do rather than being a problem with your product or service. The key threads of consistency and persistence run through this book and should run through your business.

Time to unleash your inner diva

When we are marketing, we are sharing what we have with the world. To help you do this, I invite you to find and unleash your inner diva. She is that part of you that is fierce; she expects and she receives because she knows it is her right and is confident in what she has to offer the world. This isn't about becoming someone new, it's about rediscovering that part of you that has been pushed back and silenced over the years. Now is the time to talk to your inner diva and find out:

- Who is she?
- How does she act in the world?
- What does she wear?
- What does she expect?
- What is she open to receive?

Beyoncé famously has her own alter ego, Sasha Fierce, a persona she liked to embody when she was performing, who was more confident and bolder than she felt herself to be. It's an interesting idea to play with. Could you base your decisions and expectations on your inner diva? If this sounds like a stretch then good, it's past time.

Open to receive

The Good Girl personality is a giver, not a taker, but when it comes to marketing your business, you need to be open to receive. I know that I struggle with this part and that at times I've been closed down, with all my energy going outwards, towards others, not open to it coming back to me. When talking at a networking event I was much more likely to deflect and ask questions than to share more about myself and my business.

Unleashing your inner diva is the start of this process of being open to receive and remembering that you're the answer to someone's prayers; your product or service is a real solution for others. Perhaps you handmake jewellery and you sell something personalised and thoughtful that makes a great gift. Maybe you, like me, support women to teach them how to grow a profitable and sustainable business faster with fewer mistakes. If you don't have that self-belief yet, stay open to it. To have a successful business that draws people to what you do, that energy needs to start with you.

Your message

Have you ever created a product or service, put it out into the world and got crickets? No response, no sales? I'm sure we all have.

Let's turn that around. On the average day, how many offers and products do you see, scroll past and not buy? Tens? Hundreds?

Most of us make the mistake of putting something out into the world once and expecting the sales to come in. Or just building the website and hoping that the traffic will come. This is not a strategy – let's sort one out for you.

We buy from people we know, like and trust

Let's get back to the psychology. People buy from people they know, like and trust. It is rare that customers buy from you the first time they discover you. Many will want to do their research, check whether you are a legitimate business and get to know you first. The research stats vary but the average number of touch points is eight. If someone has never heard of you and stumbles across you, it is likely that the number will be a lot higher.[51]

Any interaction between your potential customer and your business is a touch point. If you think about what marketers call the customer journey, typically a customer will discover you on social media, visit your website and look at some products, check out the reviews and testimonials, look at a few social media posts and then decide what to buy.

From my own experience, I've found that people are looking even if they're not interacting with you and some sales seem to come out of the blue without any interaction first. Having regular social media posts helps give people confidence that your business is still running and that buying from you is worthwhile.

What do I say?

At its heart, marketing is about saying 'here it is, buy it now', but you need to share more than that. We need to build up our 'know, like and trust' through our messaging.

EXERCISE: Planning your content

Whether it's on the social media platform(s) of your choice or via email, it's good to have some topics to help you structure what you are sharing. Think about what these mean to you and then start writing down your ideas for these main topic areas:

- **Storytelling and identity:** Your business journey, a day in the life, who you work with, what matters to you.

- **Educational**: How to use your product/service, tips, hacks, case studies, behind the scenes, answering common questions.
- **Selling**: Products, offers, testimonials.
- **Community and engagement**: Ask questions, start conversations, giveaways, challenges.
- **Inspirational**: Aspirational images and quotes, relevant lifestyle topics, recommended books.

I like to have a document on my computer, or you may have notes in your phone for this. Write down all the ideas that come to you around these five topic areas and keep adding to the list. This is a great way to ensure that you have a breadth of content so you're not one-dimensional.

Connection is key

When someone buys from a small business it is not the same as buying from a big brand and that is a good thing for you. As an example, think about something you've bought from a small business. If someone were to ask you about it, what would you say?

If I purchased a gold necklace as a present for a family member from Homebird Jewellery, I would say: 'I bought this personalised necklace from Jess of Homebird Jewellery. She handmakes jewellery with a message and she was so great at ensuring I had something that represented her. It was brilliant to be able to gift something so unique and Jess is so lovely to buy from. I'm going to buy all my gifts from her!'

Once you've done that, have a think about what you would want someone to say about you and your business. This is a great opportunity to ask friends, family or previous customers to answer this question as that will likely give you a great steer towards the types of content to share to help connect with like-minded people.

Where to share your message

Having a website, an email list and one or more social media channels is important for small businesses.

Website

Having a website is a non-negotiable. Even if you mostly sell in person, a portfolio website is still a must as it's the first thing that someone is going to look for when considering working with you.

Social media

The number of social media channels can be overwhelming but the key thing to consider is where your ideal customer is hanging out. When you are planning your social media posts and email content you can repurpose across the platforms if you decide to use more than one, so you don't have to reinvent the wheel every time.

Photos

Particularly if you sell online (but this now goes for anyone with a website or social media), good-quality photos are not just a nice-to-have anymore, they are a must-have. I believe this is the first thing you should invest in because it makes such a big difference to the perception of your business. There are many amazing freelance photographers you can work with to get photos of you and your products. Ask your business friends for recommendations.

Email list

Email marketing is my jam. I have worked for several years growing a business, from being the first employee to six- and seven-figure years, and all of that time my job has been to do the email marketing. It is so satisfying to send one email and make tens of thousands of pounds from it.

Firstly, email has consistently been *the* place to make sales for several years and I don't see that changing. When someone signs up to receive your emails it's a sign that they are truly interested in what you do, so your email list are your people.

Secondly, you own your email list. Social media platforms can change, and you could even lose your account. That can't happen with email.

This is a radical statement I know, but you need to send emails to your list. Even when your list is just a couple of family members, send emails as though you have thousands of subscribers. It's a mindset thing, but take it seriously whatever the size.

Work out how often you can email your list and stick to it. Is it weekly, twice a month, monthly? Whatever works for you do that. Don't just email when you have a product to promote – that's like a friend only getting in touch around their birthday, it's transparent. We want to stay connected with our people and share updates and stories.

The Good Girl in you might be bristling right now. As with everything marketing, this can feel like a big deal. What I want you to remember is that this is *your* business. If you have a Good Girl personality, I can guarantee that what you sell – whether it's a product or a service – is well thought through and it's something that people either want or need or both. You are not bothering people by sharing something that they want.

The importance of launches

Launching products or services and limited-time offers is a great strategy to use. If you think about it, when something is always available there is no real urgency to buy it, but if you work with one-off products, limited-time programmes, etc then your customer needs to make a decision – are they in or not?

Sharing just before your launch that something is coming, regularly sharing during the launch and then repeatedly reminding people of the deadline is the way to do it. I can guarantee that if you do it right, you will feel like you're bothering people and you will still get people saying that they didn't realise you have a launch going on! People do not see everything you put out into the world so you need to repeat yourself regularly in order for people to hear you.

Data-led decision-making

With all of your marketing efforts, it's important to trial things, check what is working and then do more of that. The 'checking what is working' part is the crucial step that is easy to miss. We can end up just making more of what we like without stepping back and reflecting on what is working.

How do we know what's working?

With social media posts, check your insights. What type of content is getting the most views, engagement and link clicks?

For email marketing, which emails are getting the highest open rates and click-through rates?

Your success will always be about switching it up and trying different approaches, but when you hit on something that's working, try to replicate it.

Developing your sales mindset

Being bold with your marketing means that you need to sell what you do. Many people find the idea of selling a bit 'icky' and distasteful. This is likely because the only time we remember being sold to is when that experience was pushy or manipulative. Look around you right now. I'm willing to bet that you've bought things that are in your eyeline happily when the selling has been done well.

This was something I knew I wanted to work on for myself, so I hired Anna Payne as my coach. Anna is the author of the bestseller, *Everything You've Been Taught About Sales is Wrong (Probably)* – a book I recommend.[52] I have learnt many things from Anna and the ethos I like to follow is to 'attract and offer' rather than 'push and close'.

When I'm sharing my services, I want to attract the right people to me and offer them a win-win, a real no-brainer. I don't want to push people to buy from me or use 'closing' or persuasion techniques to try to 'make' people buy. I truly believe that if it feels forced, you just end up with customers and clients who felt manipulated to purchase rather than those truly excited to work with you, and that always ends badly.

You don't have to do this alone. The global market-place – marketing in particular – is ever-evolving. Something that worked last year may not work now. Marketing has been my job for over a decade and I've been an integral part of growing a business from zero to million-pound years. Bold marketing is one of the main areas that I support the Good Girls with, whether in a group programme or one to one. Check out goodgirlrebellion.com/book for my most up-to-date support, free guides and shortcuts.

Summary

- 'Closed mouths don't get fed.'[53] It's time to share what you have to offer.

- Unleash your inner diva to regularly share what you have to offer in a myriad of different ways and be open to receive.

- Having a website, social media profiles and email list are non-negotiables for business now.

- Launching offers and products is a great way to get sales.

- Email is a key channel, so email your list regularly, no matter what the size.

- It is key to check what is working with data-led decision-making.

Now to the second 'e' in our REBEL methodology: empowered pricing – looking at how your money mindset impacts yourself and your business and how to get pricing just right.

8

Empowered Pricing

The second 'E' in the REBEL methodology is empowered pricing. There are so many amazing women giving up well-paid jobs to work in their own business, only to end up working more hours for less pay. While money may not be your only motivating factor, it should be one of them. In this chapter we'll be diving into your money mindset, how that is impacting you and your business, and ensuring that you are pricing correctly.

A quick note before we start. Money issues can have deep roots in the past, so go gently with yourself. There are some exercises in this chapter that encourage you to investigate some of that past. If they might be triggering for you, just skip over them for now. You can always come back to them when you're ready and the time is right.

Your money mindset

Research has found that your fundamental approach to money is formed by the time you are seven years old.[54] If money is an area that you have issues with, know that it is not your fault. Now may be the right time as an adult to deep dive into these issues and make some changes. This is important because the way we think about money affects so much of who we are, particularly how we do business. Getting curious about your money mindset is the first step to changing it, so let's start with how to do that.

Childhood messages around money

Let's have a look at the messages you got about money when you were growing up. These may have been overt (the things that were said about money) as well as implied (for example, how money was spent). You will also have picked up on other cues, behaviours and attitudes to money from your parents or caregivers. Children are astute and can read the energy and emotions of those around them before they understand what is causing them.

What messages did you get about money when you were growing up? Did you hear phrases about lack of money, such as:

- 'Money doesn't grow on trees.'

- 'We can't afford that.'

- 'Do you think I'm made of money?'

- 'Save your pennies for a rainy day.'

Or did you hear messages of abundance, such as:

- 'Money is meant to be enjoyed.'

- 'When you do what you love, the money follows.'

- 'We can find a way to afford that.'

- 'There are always ways to make more money.'

While your family income is a factor in this, it's not everything. A millionaire can be a miser with a scarcity mindset, worrying about every penny they spend, while someone on a low income can have an abundance mindset, believing that they have enough to do the things they want to do. It's interesting to reflect on these messages from childhood and how they may be affecting you now as an adult.

Wherever you're at, whether you are in a scarcity mindset or tend towards an abundance mindset, you can continue to open up more to the idea of abundance. Here are some steps to help you shift your money mindset. This is something that goes deep, so it will take time and conscious effort to change, but it is worth it.

**EXERCISE: Identify and rewrite
your limiting beliefs**

This exercise is worth doing for any limiting belief
you hold, but we'll focus on ones around money
now. Get your journal out and earmark a few pages
for this. You're going to work on identifying your
beliefs around money and you'll reframe them if you
need to.

1. Think about a belief or judgement you have
    about money.

2. Write down the opposite of that belief.

3. Reflect on how you feel when you receive,
    spend or ask for money. What emotions come
    up? What stories or fears come to mind and
    where might those come from?

4. With all the reflections from steps 1 to 3, what is
    a more empowering and supportive belief that
    you can choose?

Here are a few examples to get you started:

-   'I'm not good with money' *becomes* 'I am learning
    to manage and grow my money wisely.'

-   'Money is the root of all evil' *becomes* 'Having
    money enables generosity, security and allows
    me to support the causes that I love.'

-   'Making money is hard' *becomes* 'There are
    many ways to grow wealth, and I can find
    opportunities that play to my strengths.'

When you are writing the opposite and reframing
for a more empowering thought, it needs to be

something you can believe right now. For example, 'I'm not good with money' doesn't become 'I am great with money' because that is too far from what you believe now. 'I am learning to manage and grow my money wisely' is true. You are reading this book, you are growing a business and you have the opportunity to expand into an abundance mindset.

At the end of each day, read your reframed thoughts, preferably out loud. Your mind cannot tell the difference between something imagined and something real, hence why you can feel anxious about something that isn't even happening, so getting into the habit of reading your new, more empowering thoughts does start to rewire your brain.

Once you've read your thoughts, take a minute to be grateful for what the money you have has done for you today. For example, I am grateful for the food that I bought today, for the coffee I had, for the money that I have in my bank account. As mentioned in Chapter 4, gratitude is the antidote to fear. It helps you notice more of the positives than the negatives in your life.

EXERCISE: Looking to the future

Now that you've started looking at where you are with your money mindset, it's time to expand your money vision. Take ten minutes and write out your responses to the following.

If money was no issue:

- What would I do?
- What would I buy?
- What would I stop doing?

These questions are about expanding your mind and your thinking. We can get stuck in a rut, thinking a lot of the same thoughts as yesterday, so imagining your future is a great way to refocus on what you want.

Spend time around people who think abundantly

If you can find a networking group nearby, it is worth going along. Finding people that view money differently to you is eye-opening and brain expanding. Look out for my latest group programme, which will be full of inspiring women like you (go to goodgirlrebellion .com/book for all the up-to-date information).

MY STORY: Changing my money mindset

I recently invested in a one-year mastermind with a sales specialist. I knew that I needed to continue to expand my own money mindset and this was a great way to do it. It was inspiring to be a part of a group of amazing businesswomen making big moves and big sales. Frankly, it was intimidating at times, but it was invaluable in challenging beliefs I didn't even realise I had about money and selling.

The gender pay gap in self-employment

We can all agree that the gender pay gap is wrong and that women should be paid equally to men for doing the same job. Despite laws and decades of campaigns, this gap remains.

There's something more. Again and again, research shows that self-employed women are not charging in the same way as men for a similar or better product or service. In the UK, research shows that men charge an average of 43% more than self-employed women and the gap in employment is 17%.[55] In the US, research by ZenBusiness found that male freelancers charge 48% more than female freelancers.[56]

Let's allow that to sink in. Even when we're in control of our pricing, we're not charging correctly and the gender pay gap exists. This is my current obsession. If you are looking hard at yourself right now and know that this is you, know that I don't blame you for it. It's up to all of us to rectify this, one person at a time, starting with yourself.

Disruptive idea – charge what you're worth

This shouldn't be a disruptive idea, yet many of us are not charging what we're worth so perhaps it is. I say this with love, but you need to value what you do and charge appropriately. If you don't, you don't have a business, you have an expensive hobby.

If you know that you're not charging correctly right now, that's fine. You can see from the statistics that you are far from the only one, so let's not get caught up in self-recrimination. When we know better, we do better. We're going to look at why we don't charge correctly, how to price what we do and how to put up our prices.

Why do we undercharge?

Good Girl personalities undercharge for one or more of the following reasons:

- **'I really enjoy what I do. This is a passion project, it's not about the money.'** I worked extensively with handmade jewellers since 2010 and makers and artists often have this reaction, particularly when the income source starts out as a hobby. It's as though we shouldn't enjoy our work and get paid well for it! Or work is only work if it includes struggle and boredom. That is not the case. If you need it, here is permission to enjoy what you do and get paid well for it.

- **'I don't need to make money from this.'** When someone has a side hustle that they start for fun, maybe they don't need to make money from it to begin with and sometimes it stays that way. If that side hustle is ever going to turn into a business that can fund the lifestyle you want to live – and perhaps ultimately your retirement – you need to price correctly and you need to do that now. Your time and effort is worth it, whether it's your main job or not.

- **'I'm not good enough yet to charge more.'** This is imposter syndrome and a lack of self-worth in disguise. It sounds sensible but it's not. When people start out, they often want to charge less or give away their products or services, but this can lead to issues down the line. If and when you want to make this your main income, you will have to put your prices up, and doing this is much harder than bringing them down.

The consequences for others

If the consequences for yourself aren't a big deal for you, I urge you to think of the consequences of not charging correctly for the wider community. Undercharging for what you do affects others whose livelihoods depend on it. Back to my original example, if someone is making and selling jewellery, only charging for the materials and not charging for their labour, then they are undercutting jewellers who are making a living from what they do. This also affects the market as a whole and the perception customers have about the value of the products or services you sell. If you don't want the money, charge correctly for it and give the profit to charity.

Role model

You are a role model for the people around you and you teach them how to treat you. If you are working for free or devalue what you do, what message is that giving your children, friends and family? Would you be happy if your daughter, niece or granddaughter was working hard but not valuing their work or charging correctly? Would you be willing to work for someone else, make them money and not be paid?

Charging correctly is important, and the next section is all about how to do that.

How to price correctly

This all sounds good, but what are the practical steps you can take to price your product or service correctly? There are some calculations to do, and you can find a free step-by-step guide to pricing for product-based businesses and service businesses on my website at goodgirlrebellion.com/book.

Something interesting happens when we do these calculations. If you got a bit scared of the price you should be charging, there are a few reasons for this.

You may not be your ideal customer

One thing that can halt your progress is doing a pricing calculation and thinking 'well, I wouldn't pay that' and then putting the price down because of it. We are all guilty of it. I know I was until I had this experience:

MY STORY: Imposter syndrome pricing

I have previously had a jewellery business and was commissioned to make a necklace by a famous actor. The necklace was for his famous wife, and it was a real thrill to be asked. Enter the imposter syndrome and not knowing how to price it! I set a cost based on the cost of materials and an hourly rate for the time I thought it would take to make. Of course, it took much longer, and I hadn't priced it right. When

the customer received it they were so thrilled they paid me more than I asked for!

We all hope for those kinds of customers but the whole experience taught me something valuable. I wouldn't have paid the amount that I was charging at that time, but I was not my ideal customer. My customer was a man who had an unlimited budget and was looking for a wgift that was personalised and exclusive. They valued that I was able to make it for them and their perception of what they wanted to spend on their wife's birthday was different to any budget I might have ever had!

Price and value

The price of your work signals to your potential customers the value of what you are selling. If your price is too low, the perception is that there must be something wrong with it or you must be cutting corners. When they compare you to your competitors, they may conclude that your product or service must be inferior, and you will miss out on sales.

Unrealistic pricing can also lead to attracting the wrong kinds of customers. Those that are price sensitive will tend to shop around and go for the cheapest option and will not have loyalty to you and your business. You don't need those types of customers.

You have so much to bring to the world through your business and you deserve an income that you're excited to get, not just something that is adequate. Pricing is about the numbers and calculation, yes, but pricing *correctly* is about your self-worth.

How to increase your prices

I've convinced you that you need to put your prices up, but how do you do it?

You can approach it in two ways. If you want to, you can announce that a price increase is coming and make some additional sales now. I recently did that with my teaching business. An increase in costs meant that I needed to increase my workshop prices, but I announced it in advance and told people they could book at the current price until a certain date. This led to a sharp increase in sales for those who had been thinking about booking but hadn't yet. The alternative is to quietly put up your prices – I can almost guarantee that no one will notice.

Summary

- Our money mindset is set by the age of seven. You may have a scarcity or an abundance mindset.

- How we view money will impact how we do business.

- There is a gender pay gap in self-employment and it is a true act of rebellion to charge what you're worth.

- Your price is an indication to your potential customer of your worth and the value of what you do.

- Good Girl personalities undercharge. Regularly review your pricing and don't hesitate to put your prices up when you need to, either with an announcement or quietly.

The next chapter explores the final tenet of our REBEL methodology: liberating results – the signs that you are on the right path in your Good Girl Rebellion.

9

Liberating Results

If you're doing what has been outlined in this book so far, even imperfectly, you will see results. To start with, it will just be glimmers; little signs that you are on the right track. If you can keep going with your everyday action, these small glimmers will start to become wins and you will build momentum. Your Good Girl Rebellion is happening.

These results are what we are working towards. The sales coming in, the right customers/clients finding you and the joy of working with them. The money is enough for you to quit the day job and go all in. Liberating results is about how we keep growing and deal with the setbacks that can come up along the way so that progress is inevitable.

It's time to get strategic

It's easy to work *in* our business – by that I mean we can get on with day-to-day tasks. It can feel like we're running in the hamster wheel and getting things done. The dopamine hit of the little wins is great, but as the CEO of our own businesses we need to be strategic, set our direction and make some bold decisions. I don't know about you, but at times I find big decisions and goal setting loom large in my brain and can mean holding back. What if it's the wrong goal and the wrong direction?

To grow a profitable business, we also need to work *on* our business and take a strategic approach. This means regularly taking a step back to look at it as a whole to ensure you are still heading in the right direction. One of the ways to work both on and in your business is by regularly reflecting and setting goals.

Where does our reluctance to commit to goals come from?

I was coaching a client recently who told me in an almost offhand way about a big goal that she had. We talked about the goal, and I could see that deep down she knew she wanted to work on it but was just not doing it. It had become a block and she was doing anything and everything to avoid it, including taking on voluntary work. The project was large with a lot of parts that needed some consistent time and attention to get it going. There was no quick win, but the potential payoff would be huge. Yet it continued to be on her list of 'things I should really get to', with no progress being made towards it. Sound familiar? Hearing what she had to say sounded like an echo of what I have in my head too.

I spent the hour of our session drilling into where the reluctance was coming from and her reasons were as follows:

- **'No one's told me it's the right decision.'** Good Girls are excellent at working for others and getting things done but deciding on our own goals can be difficult. After all, there are so many ways to go about achieving the same ends. Our high empathy makes us big-picture thinkers with a wide vision, which means it can be hard to pick a path from all the options. This is where having a coach can be helpful, because in that hour we were able to pick it apart, blast away the blocks and plan to move forwards.

- **'I don't have a deadline.'** We always meet external deadlines, but when it's our own deadline, suddenly the impetus is not there. Chapter 3 is the solution to this, and the sooner you find innovative ways to get external accountability, the faster you will grow.

- **'This is a big and very visible project. Am I the right person to do it?'** When we got into it, we found a lack of self-belief. I've talked a lot about this in Chapter 5, but I want to bring it in again here to remind you that this isn't about logic. The person I was coaching is supremely capable of making a huge success of this big project she's shying away from.

How do we get it done?

I propose that having one big scary goal each year is a good thing to aim for. It's usually something you know is going to be a turning point for your business but is a risk if it doesn't pay off. That could be a financial risk, but it may also be a risk in terms of an investment of your time and energy.

> **MY STORY: A risk that didn't pay off**
>
> I spent about fifteen months developing the Good Girl Rebellion app. Becoming an app developer is not as easy as I'd hoped; it isn't the same as creating an online course, there are additional levels of complexity. When the Good Girl Rebellion app made it to the Apple App Store and the Google Play Store I was elated. It was a journey of over a year, and it didn't sell.
>
> I was working with my own coach and talking with her about it. We reviewed it and found that it had

too much content. It sounds counterintuitive but it did have everything I'd learnt in it and those that started it didn't finish because it was overwhelming.

I found keeping up with all the regulations of being an app developer too much. It was always the thing that went to the bottom of my to-do list and then there was a scramble when the deadlines hit to share this bit of paperwork or that piece of information.

The annual fee for renewing the app was looming and I just felt like I was on the wrong track; not with the content but with the app as a way of delivering it. I shut it all down. Perhaps if I'd stopped and reflected more along the way I wouldn't have gone down that path. Equally I can say that I learnt a lot, that a lot of the content of the app is in this book and I was able to develop my ideas more clearly because of it.

Taking a calculated risk is always worthwhile. It may pay off, but even if it doesn't you will end up further in your business with new insights.

Goal setting

There's enough written about SMART (specific, measurable, achievable, realistic, time-bound) targets that I don't want to reiterate, but it is important for your goals to be all of these things.

I have personally found goal setting a challenge. Many people talk about setting a target that is a stretch, but how much of a stretch? Rather counterintuitively, I can be demotivated by goals that feel so big I don't know where to start. Here is a solution.

Setting goal levels

Think about setting three levels for your goals:

1. The minimum it would take for you to feel like you'd achieved the goal. Let's say your goal was around the income from a launch, Level 1 is the number that would make you feel like you had made it. For example, if I am running a launch I might be aiming for five sales or £10k in revenue.

2. What would be an even better result? I might aim for eight sales and £16k in revenue at Level 2.

3. These are the champagne goals (with thanks to Anna Payne for this idea). What result would be so great that you would get the champagne out? For me, Level 3 would be fifteen sales and £30k in revenue.

This is a great way to reframe the idea of stretch targets. In the early 2000s I had what was my only corporate job and they were big fans of stretch targets, but when a target felt like too much of a stretch, I was actually demotivated. I'd be sure it was too high, that I couldn't reach that goal. When you set up the levels of your goal it is more expansive. If you get your five sales in the first week, you have your next level goals to keep you moving forwards.

I saw a great idea for making this concept even more powerful. Someone bought champagne bottles and wrote a goal on each label so it was ready for opening when the goal was achieved – a visual representation of what you want to achieve and your expectation that you'll achieve it.

Quarterly planning

Many businesses suggest quarterly planning. While you, like me, may be leaving a corporate career behind, I think this is smart. A quarter of a year is three months – around ninety days – a good amount of time to get a significant project done, but not so long that you have time to procrastinate.

Going back to our productivity, discussed in Chapter 5, I don't believe we should fill every quarter with action. One of the benefits of having your own business is working with your own rhythms. If the first quarter of the year is a time for hibernation for you, why not schedule something that suits that vibe? If you have children, the summer holidays may mean an extended period of time where you are limited in what you do for your business. Knowing and planning for this in advance is great for you and the longevity of your business. We are not machines, and the ultimate rebellion is to do business your way.

Urgent versus important

When a CEO I worked for in my corporate job announced, 'This year we're going to focus on the important things, not the urgent things,' it stayed with me. By their very nature, urgent things are urgent and we do them first! That can lead to the important things that will make a difference to the business, like the project my coaching client was avoiding, being left behind. When you are considering what to focus on, it is crucial to take that longer-term view and balance the urgent and important. If you can make what is important urgent, you've cracked the code of true business growth.

If you reflect right now on your immediate and longer-term plans, how can you ensure that both are getting done?

MY STORY: Redefining success

I hope you will have identified throughout this book that I believe that success is whatever you define it as.

I remember back to a time, probably fifteen years ago, when I wanted to have more time freedom.

I was working as a full-time teacher and I was exhausted. The idea of being able to work part time, enjoy what I was doing and fill my time with the things that bring me joy felt alien, yet that was what I wanted.

I can reflect now on what I have. My businesses both continue to grow and my earning is many times higher than when I worked as a full-time teacher. I just found out yesterday that I have won a business award. Life is good and continues to get better.

Success does not have to be one-dimensional. It is true rebellion to strive for enough money, fulfilment, joy, connection, free time. Reflect on what this means for you.

Personal fulfilment goals

If you want to build and grow your business, I am willing to bet that you have a passion for what you do and you want the freedom to set your own work hours, perhaps work from wherever you want (depending on your business). The money is important but it's not just about the money. I encourage you to write down your personal fulfilment goals.

EXERCISE: Your personal fulfilment goals

Here are some of the key areas of personal fulfilment. Get your journal out and think about each one in turn. Write down at least one goal for each of these (hopefully you will have more):

- Experiences and travel
- Dream purchases
- Personal growth and education
- Health and wellness
- Family, relationships and social life
- Giving and impacting

Whatever your goal is, write it down, even if it might seem trivial or silly to someone else. It doesn't have to make sense to others – the more trivial and sillier the better! This is about what motivates you. You don't have to show this to anyone but keeping track of these goals – big and small – will help you stay motivated in those moments where you need a boost.

Dealing with setbacks

It is inevitable that things won't always go your way. You'll work hard on a launch and it will fall flat. You'll share a social media post you worked hard on and get crickets.

There is one question that I've found to genuinely change my outlook on anything: Why is this the best thing that could have happened?

I mentioned earlier that I recently had a launch that didn't sell as well as I'd hoped. I had done a lot of work on it and I was disappointed that the work hadn't panned out. I asked myself, 'Why is this the best thing that could have happened?' I found that I could think of lots of great reasons:

- It allowed me to take some time off and have a break, which I may not have had capacity for.

- It allowed me to rethink the offer and find something better.

- It allowed me the time to reflect on whether I am moving in the right direction with my business.

I often like to give myself a little wallowing time and feel sorry for myself. Once that is past, asking this question always gives me a new perspective.

When should I give up the day job?

This is a question that comes up regularly. I see people on social media sharing stories about giving up their day job to pursue their passion, going all in on their business, leap and the net will appear, etc. I'm sure you've heard these kinds of messages too. I know there are success stories out there that start with this story but there are some questions to ask yourself first. Crucially, I don't think it's the only way to grow a business.

Here are some questions to ponder.

Financial constraints

Is it financially viable for me to give up my day job right now?

I went to a talk at the Edinburgh Book Festival with the amazing writer Steven Moffat and he was talking about how the only barrier to getting into TV writing is now socio-economic. He said that money was more important than class, gender, race or other factors and that those that had financial backing from family were able to take voluntary positions and get a foot in the door that those without financial support could not sustain. I have worked part time while building my business and I can acknowledge this means that the growth will have been slower than if I'd been able to go all in full time on it.

There is evidence that women can struggle to get venture capital for their businesses, if they want to go down that route. For example, the Women Entrepreneurs Finance Initiative (We-Fi) report states that women-led businesses get significantly less financial support, and women are perceived as high-risk borrowers.[57]

If we have a financial cushion, we have more freedom and time to grow the business faster. We have money to invest in support, development and staffing. Without that, we will likely need to keep the day job until the scales tip and the business is earning the same or more than the day job.

Your attitude to risk

Am I willing to take the risk to quit the day job right now?

This goes hand in hand with financial constraints but is a slightly different consideration. Your attitude to risk is important and will likely be affected by your life experiences to date as well as your psychology. It also depends on your confidence in finding a job if you end up needing one again.

I am very risk averse and I am also the main earner in my household. Both of these things have meant that I have not been a 'leap and the net will appear' kind of person. I envy those that are.

Does it have to be either/or?

What other options are there?

Sometimes we can think in black-and-white terms and there may be options we haven't considered. Could you reduce your hours or take a sabbatical to work on the business?

> **MY STORY: Taking a sabbatical**
>
> When I first moved from London to Edinburgh, I took a one-year sabbatical from my teaching job. I needed that cushion and the ability to go back if it didn't work out for me. It did work out and I never went back to the teaching job, but I did need the possibility of going back before I was confident to move forward and try something new.

Let's ease up on the pressure to choose

Rather than putting the pressure on, what if there is a natural moment, coming soon, where the scales tip and it's a no-brainer? When that happens, you will definitely know.

Don't buy into the story that you're not taking your business seriously if you don't risk it all. As with everything, the only thing you need to do is what feels right in this moment.

Summary

- The results of your Good Girl Rebellion will come in glimmers first, and you'll know you're on the right track.

- Work on one exciting yet scary goal each year.

- Try goal setting at three different levels and see what you can achieve.

- Planning your focus so you have one big task to do per quarter helps ensure your business is moving forwards.

- Remember to do the important as well as the urgent tasks.

- Get clear on your personal fulfilment goals as they can be as motivating or more than money goals.

- Defining success by your own terms is an act of true rebellion.

- Asking 'Why is this the best thing that could have happened?' is the key to dealing with setbacks.

PART THREE
THE GOOD GIRL LEADER

Right now, you are likely in a space between where you were and where you want to be. This is an exciting place to be but at times it can be daunting. This is where we need to draw on our new-found knowledge of how to manage ourselves, our persistence and our vision of what is to come in order to keep moving forward one step at a time.

Part Three has some mini pep talks for you to turn to when you need them. We'll also be looking at how you step into the Good Girl Leader role you were always meant to have. I'll be waving my magic wand to let you know all of my dreams for you and your future.

10

Mistakes, Myths And Momentum

Now you know what to do to grow your dream business and dream life. This chapter covers some key thoughts and worries that have come from my clients' experiences as they move through this stage of their business growth. There are some big mistakes we make that hold us back. There are some myths it's time to bust. How do we build the momentum we need to make it easy? These are mini pep talks waiting for you when you need them.

Here is the list of pep talks in this chapter. Do flick forward to the one that you need right now:

- **Support**: 'My friends and family don't understand my dream. I don't have any support.'

- **Vision and clarity**: 'I just get so excited about all of the possibilities that are ahead of me. I want to stay open to all these great opportunities because I don't want to miss out on anything.'

- **Action**: 'I feel like I've been slogging hard for a long time and it's just not happening for me. Maybe it's time to give up this dream. It's not working.'

- **Giving up**: 'I want to grow my business but it takes so much hard work to make money. Maybe I should just give up and work for someone else; it feels less risky.'

- **Feeling stuck**: 'I feel stuck. I don't know what to do next.'

- **Self-promotion**: 'I know I need to be bold and get my business out there, but I fear that level of visibility and self-promotion gives me the 'ick'.'

- **Visibility**: 'I hate social media. I just feel drained by it. It's so fake and such a waste of time.'

- **Comparison**: 'She's doing better than me. I'll never catch up.'

- **Failure**: 'What if I fail?'

- **Success**: 'What if I succeed?'

Support

- **The thought**: 'My friends and family don't understand my dream. I don't have any support.'

- **The mistake**: Allowing lack of support to undermine your belief in yourself and your business.

- **The path**: It's time to find the support you need.

I hope this is not your story and that you have many supportive and loving people surrounding you in your life, but I know that isn't always the case. I've coached a few clients who were feeling held back by the judgement of those around them, so here is some advice for you to consider.

Firstly, I am sorry to hear this. I am in your corner and if you've read this far into the book then you are definitely motivated and ready to grow a business. I am cheering you on.

While it is great to be supported, this may be your first and most important act of rebellion because you don't need someone else's permission to grow your business. If someone in your life is neutral or hostile about it, don't try to persuade them. Your energy is much better served in working on your business, getting the sales and proving that you can do it.

Secondly, remember that you are changing. The act of rebellion and growing your own business when you have spent your life working for someone else or caring for your family can be concerning and perhaps even scary for people around you. You can get hit with what Martha Beck calls the 'change-back attack'.[58] This is where people get scared that you will outgrow them and that you are changing too much so they try to make you go back to the person that you were.

From your perspective, this can feel infuriating because you don't want to be that person anymore and you feel like you're evolving into who you're meant to be. For a moment, see it from their perspective and realise that they think they're losing you. That is not to say you should conform to their outdated vision of you, but using that well-developed empathy that you have, find some understanding for their perspective and then keep growing your business. You may need to set boundaries around talking about your business with certain people and you do not need to justify yourself.

Finally, you need to find your people. If they are not within your circle of loved ones that is unfortunate, but we are out here! Find a local networking group that you can meet with regularly. Join one of the Good Girl Rebellion group programmes (for the latest information go to goodgirlrebellion.com/book). Find the community that has your back. To really grow, hang out with people, whether in person or virtually, that are a few steps ahead of you. This helps expand your vision of what is possible for you and your business, and they will know of opportunities they can share with you.

Vision and clarity

- **The thought**: 'I just get so excited about all of the possibilities that are ahead of me. I want to stay open to all these great opportunities because I don't want to miss out on anything.'

- **The mistake**: You go off in too many directions, set yourself too many goals and end up achieving none of them.

- **The path**: Focus.

This is a common issue for Good Girl Rebels. We are great at big-picture thinking and can come up with lots of different ways to solve the same problem.

The answer to this issue is to pick a project to work on for twelve weeks and go all in. Forsake all others. If an idea for something else won't go away, write it down and get back to it later. This can feel difficult, especially when you're setting up a business. There always seems to be so much to do simultaneously, but try not to get pulled in all directions. Spend twelve weeks building out your website, twelve weeks developing your product range, twelve weeks focusing on your social media and email marketing. This will move you further forward than bits and pieces here and there.

It is likely that you are at the beginning stages of your business and you have competing demands on your time, but the key is still focus. Where possible, you need to have your main focus, energy and attention on that endeavour.

'Why twelve weeks?' you may ask. As I mentioned in the previous chapter, the business world often breaks the year down into quarters, which roughly equate to twelve weeks. It's a good amount of time to get something done but it's not never-ending. If you give yourself twelve weeks to do a big task, you have to get on with it.

Action

- **The thought**: 'I feel like I've been slogging hard for a long time and it's just not happening for me. Maybe it's time to give up this dream. It's not working.'

- **The mistake**: You give up before it starts getting good.

- **The path**: Persistence. Keep going.

Do you feel like you're working hard but not seeing the results? I get it. There is a lot that goes on behind the scenes to get a business up and running. I like to think of it as invisible architecture. These are the building blocks of your business, and they need to be built before we can make significant sales. Growth is rarely linear. It reminds me of the adage that the last thing to grow on an apple tree is the fruit (with thanks to my coach Heidi Hinda Chadwick for sharing that one).

My first piece of advice is to remember to build in some external accountability for your goals (look back to Chapter 3): announce what you're doing, hire a coach, join a group. This has been a game changer for me because it's made what's in my head real. People outside of me know about my goals and dreams and they are supportive and waiting for me to make them happen.

Secondly, you need to relentlessly keep your 'ta-da' list because it's easy to focus on the thing that isn't done. We need to stop and remember the things we *have* achieved.

EXERCISE: The rebel reflection

Right now, in this moment, I'd like you to set a timer for five minutes and write down all the things you have done to grow your business up until now.

Look at that list and allow yourself to feel all of that groundwork you've already put in.

I actually stopped writing and did that exercise for myself and there were lots of things – big and small – many of which I'd forgotten about! It is a good reminder and makes me think of a cartoon I once saw of a person digging a tunnel, mining for diamonds. They'd dug a long way into the ground and couldn't see it but they were almost through to a massive cache of diamonds. If they gave up and stopped digging, they'd never know how close they were.

Building momentum for any task takes time, and at the beginning it seems like a real uphill struggle. We're working hard and doing everything we need to do, usually with competing demands for our attention. Don't give up. It will become easier and the momentum will happen if you just keep going.

Giving up

- **The thought**: 'I want to grow my business but it takes so much hard work to make money. Maybe I should just give up and work for someone else; it feels less risky.'

- **The myth**: You need to work harder to make more money.

- **The path**: You need to do the right things to make more money.

In a lot of our past experiences, working harder equalled getting more. At school, the harder we studied the better we did. In the workplace, the harder we work the more likely we are to make a bonus or get a promotion. Maybe!

When it comes to our own business, it's not necessarily the case; in fact, working harder can mean burning out and getting ill. You are your biggest business asset so you can't afford for this to happen, and you don't need to. Being productive is about more than just busywork, it's about doing the things that are going to make the biggest impact on your growth and income. You need to keep moving forwards with curiosity. 'I wonder if...?' is one of my favourite questions.

Be open to being guided by others that are a few steps ahead of you. We are prone to trying to figure everything out ourselves but unfortunately trial and error involves error and scrabbling about in the dark. We don't have time to stumble on the right way to do things. We all make mistakes, but let's make fewer of them by doing the things that work. This book has hopefully given you some ideas and direction with that.

Feeling stuck

- **The thought**: 'I feel stuck. I don't know what to do next.'

- **The mistake**: Believing that you need complete clarity before you act.

- **The path**: Take the next small step.

Feeling stuck can be frustrating. Sometimes there just isn't a clear vision of what to do next. In these moments we need to take the next small step because action helps breed clarity.

Get curious and ask, 'What if I tried this?' Rather than getting stuck, curiosity will always help move you forward and then you just keep doing that. Sometimes things only make sense in hindsight, so a step-by-step approach is the only way to keep moving forward.

Self-promotion

- **The thought**: 'I know I need to be bold and get my business out there, but I fear that level of visibility and self-promotion gives me the "ick".'

- **The mistake**: You think your business is about you.

- **The path**: Focus on the customer, not on you.

You know you need your bold marketing (see Chapter 7) to get yourself out there, but you fear the visibility. This could be because it makes you uncomfortable, you fear judgement or the idea of self-promotion just feels 'icky'.

Your business isn't about you, it's about the people that you help through your products/services. By holding back, you are limiting the number of people you can serve and that does neither you nor your potential customers any good.

You are right in that what you do is not for everyone, and that is a good thing. The right people will resonate with what you have to offer and those are the people you're speaking to. Your marketing is about *how you can help*, it's not about you. If you can focus on that message, you can create a true win-win for both you and your customer.

Visibility

- **The thought**: 'I hate social media. I just feel drained by it. It's so fake and such a waste of time.'

- **The mistake**: Using social media solely as a consumer rather than as a creator.

- **The path**: See social media as a path to connecting with your ideal customers.

You don't have to love social media, but it is one of the key ways you can connect with a global audience worldwide for free. In the past, businesses tended to have a local clientele. You'd need money to set up and would probably need a physical premises that people could visit. That is no longer the case. You can connect with like-minded people from all over the world and do business with them online. We take this for granted now, but I still think this is mind-blowing.

Some clever people have designed social media in a way to keep us consuming. What you need to do is flip that and become more of a creator than a consumer. When I catch myself doomscrolling, I remember that and stop. I can use social media as a tool to connect with people who are interested in what I do and that is its value.

You don't have to dance or follow trends, unless you want to! You just need to show up as yourself. What is going to connect us to our audience is authenticity, and as a small business you have that as an advantage. The big brands don't have that opportunity and that is why they pay celebrities a lot of money to be the 'face' of their brand.

Use social media as a tool for connection for your business and be real. Your people will find you.

Comparison

- **The thought**: 'She's doing better than me. I'll never catch up.'

- **The mistake**: Believing that someone else's success takes away from your own.

- **The path**: Everyone's path is different. Stay true to yours.

It's easy to get caught up in comparing where you are with others, thinking 'she's doing better,' 'she is more experienced than me,' etc. We need to remember that what we see of others is their success and highlights. They aren't going to show all the ups and downs they've been through to get to where they are. You know your story intimately so trying to make a comparison when you don't know the whole story is wasting your energy. Every minute you spend focusing on someone else is one you're not spending on yourself, so try to minimise comparisons. Unfollow people that trigger you; make it easier to stay in your own lane.

Get curious when you notice jealousy creeping in. What is it about that person's outward success that pushes your buttons? This can be a helpful way to discover the things that really matter to you. Is it the awards? The sales? That it looks like they have an enviable work-life balance? When you see something you're jealous of it's usually an indication of something you want, and that's useful to know.

Success doesn't come from looking sideways at others, it comes from focusing on your own business and your growth. Your journey is yours and you are right on time.

Failure

- **The thought**: 'What if I fail?'

- **The mistake**: You think failure is a sign that you are not good enough and you should just give up.

- **The path**: Embrace failure, adjust and keep going.

It's interesting that we fear failure so much when actually the thing we should fear is staying stuck. I know for myself I felt like I was treading water for a long time. I was stuck not knowing where to go and not moving forwards. Looking back on it, moving anywhere would have been better than going nowhere. While I feel like I achieved nothing, being stuck felt exhausting.

What I've learnt from experience is that in business, we try things. Some things work out and others don't. If something doesn't work out it doesn't mean that you aren't capable, it just means that the way you tried didn't work. That is useful information that is still moving you forward.

Being successful isn't about avoiding failure, it's about moving forward, being open to trying new things and keeping going. Persistence is the mark of true success.

Success

- **The thought**: 'What if I succeed? What if I can't handle it?'

- **The mistake**: You think if you succeed in your business it will mean more pressure and expectations that you won't be able to handle.

- **The path**: Trust that you will grow into each new level of success and you are capable of handling everything that comes up.

If you are afraid of success, you are afraid of what that success might bring you. Perhaps it's stress, more responsibility or a bigger audience to see when things go wrong. The truth is you will evolve as your business does. You already have what it takes to succeed and anything you need to learn, you will learn on the way. You're not meant to stay where you are, you're meant to grow. You've worked for this; it's time to enjoy it.

Summary

- If you don't have the support of those around you, it's time to find the support you need. Remember, you don't need someone else's permission to grow your business, you are changing and you need to find your people.

- Focus is the key to growth. Go all in on a project for twelve weeks.

- Keep going; don't give up. Build in some external accountability for your goals and remember the things you have achieved.

- You need to do the right things to make more money. Be open to being guided by others that

6

are a few steps ahead of you and make fewer mistakes by doing the things that work.

- Take the next small step: action helps breed clarity. Curiosity will help you move forward.

- Focus on the customer, not on you. Focus your marketing on how you can help.

- See social media as a path to connecting with your ideal customers across the globe for free. Be more of a creator than a consumer and be your authentic self.

- Everyone's path is different; stay true to yours. Minimise comparisons, unfollow people that trigger you and get curious about others' success.

- Embrace failure, adjust and keep going. Try new things to move forward. Persistence is the mark of true success.

- Trust that you will grow into each new level of success and you are capable of handling everything that comes up. You will evolve as your business does.

The next chapter looks at how we can shift our mindsets from Good Girl Rebels to Good Girl Leaders.

11

Becoming The Good Girl Leader

As Good Girl personalities we make great managers, but leadership and running our own businesses is a different proposition. It is time to shift into a new way of seeing the world as a Good Girl Leader.

A leader is someone who guides the way. She influences, inspires, motivates and acts. In this chapter I'm going to ask you to reflect on some important questions about yourself and your leadership. We're going to build on everything that has come before, start to look at the larger vision you have for yourself and your business, and think about how you can step into a leadership role.

EXERCISE: Who do you want to be and where are you holding yourself back?

As Good Girls, our high empathy means that our focus is so often turned outwards to the people around us. Get your journal out as it's time to turn inwards and ask yourself this question: *As the leader of your business, and in your life in general, who and what do you want to be?*

I want you to take your time to answer this. Spend ten minutes now, wherever you are, stop reading and think. Ideally write your thoughts down, but even just thinking your responses is valuable.

For me, these are the things that came up: Energy shifter, confident, focused, magnetic, wealthy, thoughtful, a role model, full of ideas, collaborative, oversubscribed, life changing, cheerleader, amusing, zen, a leader, inspired, supported, supportive, a magnetic speaker, joyful, a bestselling author, award winning. (As an aside, one week after writing this list down, I found out I'd won a business award. There's a powerful transformation that happens when we write things down.)

Once you've come up with your list, I want you to ask yourself this question: *In what ways am I already these things?*

Don't dismiss this question because it is powerful magic. Wherever you are right now on your journey to growing your business, you have been on this path for years. You are already achieving some of these things. One step towards becoming the leader you want to be is acknowledging you are already partway there.

Spend time being grateful for all the ways you are already on this path and then you can focus on where you are headed one step at a time.

Where are you holding yourself back?

You have so much to bring to your business and for your customers/clients. You have a vision for how you can help make life brighter with your products or services. One of the biggest questions to ask yourself every day is: *Where are you holding yourself back?*

When you know where you're holding back, it's time to ask why. You may need to drill down into it and ask 'why' a few times to get to the core of the issue. What you'll likely find at the centre is fear.

As an example, I am holding back on sharing my business on social media.

Why?

Because I don't feel ready yet.

Why?

Because I don't feel like the expert I need to be yet to share about it.

Why?

Because I'm afraid of being called out, that someone will realise that I'm not confident.

These are big questions to ask, but they will move you forwards if you can ask them.

What are the thoughts that are holding you back?

How are you playing small?

Even with those fears and doubts, are you ready to stop playing small with what you want from life?

These questions come with a side order of fear, but when you're ready, it's time to do the things you're resisting doing because that is the only way through.

These, by definition, are sore spots for us, so go gently. It is great if you can identify an old belief, realise that it doesn't serve you anymore and let it go. Actually, you don't have to work through everything before you move forwards. It doesn't have to be either/or. You can be afraid of public speaking and stand up to introduce yourself. You can be an introvert and speak on a stage. You can worry about hiring staff and hire staff. That's the secret to great leadership.

Are you hyper independent?

Good Girl personalities are often hyper independent, preferring to work things out for themselves. There is a free 'Are You Hyper Independent?' quiz, which you can find at goodgirlrebellion.com/book, but for now, here are some questions to ponder:

- Do you think asking for help is admitting you're not good enough or you're failing?

- Do you struggle to delegate or outsource because no one can do it as well as you?

- Do you agree with the statement, 'It's faster if I do it myself'?

Have you delayed investing in support, e.g. coaching, a mentor or staff members, because you believed you should be able to figure it out alone?

Do you struggle to trust others with key parts of your business even though you are overwhelmed and overworked?

Do you find yourself trying to work things out that are not in your expertise rather than getting an expert to do it?

When something isn't working in your business is your instinct to push harder rather than get guidance?

Do you admire people that seem to 'do it all' and secretly think you should be the same?

If you answered yes to five or more of these questions, you are likely hyper independent. This doesn't surprise me, as it is one of the consequences of the Good Girl personality.

Here are some things to think about:

- You don't need to do it alone.

- Getting support and advice is the smartest thing to do.

- The thinking that has got you here won't get you to where you want to go.

Think about something that you are expert in; it could be a skill or a job that you have. When you start learning anything new, you don't know what you don't know. When you learn a little more, you start to find out about all the things you don't know and that can feel overwhelming. Gradually, you fill in those gaps in your knowledge and eventually become an expert yourself. In this case, our access to so much information now is to our detriment because it gives us a false sense that we can work it all out for ourselves. That makes our hyper independent hearts sing! I wonder how many of the 50% of businesses that fail within the first three years are those that are DIYing their business and give up through lack of progress. Getting the help and advice you need is a strength, not a weakness.

How can you get the support you need?

Look, Ms I-Can-Do-Everything-On-My-Own, it's time to shed that skin because you've outgrown the DIY strategies, which is why you reached for this book. The fact is every successful leader on the planet has support of some kind. Support will get you there faster and stop you giving up along the way.

Support comes in many forms. It might mean hiring freelancers or staff to handle essential tasks or outsourcing parts of your process to free up your time. It might look like collaborating with others to grow together. It should mean continuing to invest in the guidance, knowledge and mentorship that will elevate you to the next level. Having the right coach can be a game changer.

Hiring support

Depending on where you are in your business right now – whether you're right at the beginning, ready to grow and hire staff or already have staff – I want you to get into the habit of doing this.

For every task you are about to do in your business, think about whether you could delegate it. There will be tasks that only you can do in terms of growing your business and there will be tasks that others can do. Even if you're not in a position to hire anyone yet, start thinking about the tasks you can pass on to someone else in the future. Setting your systems up so that a staff member or virtual assistant could take them over is a great way to open yourself up for change.

Here are some examples to help get you thinking:

- Ensure you have template emails for FAQs. This will make it quicker for you to send out answers and it paves the way for someone else to do it in the future.

- Compile a guide on how to respond to recurring tasks for your business; for example, how to process orders. This will help save you time and brain power each time it comes up.

- Organise documents, photos and logos into online storage folders. Again, this will save you time, but it also ensures you are ready to hand tasks over to someone else.

In whose interest is it that you go it alone?

When I first asked myself this question I got chills. The fact is we've been taught to be self-sufficient. The school classroom was one of the first places where you were reinforced and praised for getting on with things quietly. As a full-time teacher myself in a previous career, I know that classroom numbers can be high and the only way for learning to happen is for the majority of students to be able to get on with their work themselves. You can do so much more when you have help, support and guidance, in terms of having expert guidance and staff to support you with the day-to-day running of the business.

I want you to ponder on this as well: In whose best interest is it to keep you from the knowledge you need to grow? Who benefits when you spend all your time trying to become an expert in something that doesn't interest you, such as learning photography to take photos of your products or learning graphic design to create a logo? Who benefits when you scrabble around hoping to land on the right action that is going to grow your business rather than getting a coach or mentor to help you get there faster?

Your competition for one. Your boss (if you're working) for another. Having to do everything ourselves is what keeps us small. Don't trick yourself into side quests, learning things you don't need to learn that take your attention away from growing the business. My friend and fellow coach Bridget Doogan was coaching me and she said something I will never forget. I was talking about the tasks that I had on my list and how I was feeling overwhelmed. She looked at me and said, 'Beware the curse of the competent woman. Just because you *can* do something doesn't mean you should.'

That is real wisdom right there. You are the CEO of your business, so it is time to take a step back from being responsive and start to look at what you are doing and why. It is time to get the help you need to get there. I would love to be a part of that support at Good Girl Rebellion, whether in one of my group programmes or as a one to one.

When do you say no to yourself?

Have you ever had this happen? If there was something I needed help with and I was thinking of asking someone for that help, I would talk myself out of it. I'd think of the person that could help me and immediately pull back and decide not to ask them. I'd worry they'd say no. I'd worry they'd be scornful. I'd worry they'd realise that I needed help and it would feel like a sign of weakness.

When we know who to ask but don't ask them, we're not even giving the person the chance to respond, which is controlling and pretty arrogant of us. Leaders ask for what they want and allow people to make their own decisions.

Who can you collaborate with?

Something I wholeheartedly believe and hope that you have gleaned from this book is that understanding ourselves is key to our success. The reason this is important is that it's not about trying to change who we are and how we act in the world; it's about finding people whose skills and outlook complement yours.

When I understood how much I benefit from collaborations and working with others who are doing their best work, things changed for me. I worked with content creators who helped me make engaging social media content, with a photographer to get great photos to share, with a jeweller to create the Good Girl Rebellion jewellery range, with Heidi to start a podcast, with a designer to create my branding and with a T-shirt designer to design merchandise.

The joy of it is that I have found that whenever we collaborate, we are always greater than the sum of our parts. While the final product is important, the magic happens in the process of working together – the conversations that spark ideas, the new avenues to explore and the results that wouldn't come without that collaboration. I am always motivated by that.

Think about the following:

- What projects would you like to bring to life?
- Who could you collaborate with to make them happen?
- What are your weaknesses and who can you hire?

We are so great at getting things done; we are competent women. You need to remember that others can do things as well as or better than you. There will come a point in your business when you are overcapacity. When it is just you there's only so much you can do.

When you start to work with freelancers and hire staff for yourself, the capacity for your business grows and so does the possibility of making more sales.

One of the best ways to start is by hiring others to do the bits of the job you don't like – hire around your weaknesses. As the CEO of your business, you want to spend the majority of your time growing the business and doing the parts that only you can do. If you are doing all the little tasks that someone else could do for you, you're not going to grow fast enough to make the profit you want. This can lead to feeling demotivated and wanting to give up before it gets good. Remember that stat from right at the beginning: 50% of businesses fail within three years? You can be in the thriving 50%, and you don't have to do it alone.[59]

Who has your back?

MY STORY: Networking

I am fortunate now to be surrounded by successful and supportive women, but when I moved from England to Scotland in 2017, I didn't know anyone here. I made a point of searching out opportunities and went to different networking events – some of them were not my scene! At others, I met people I gelled with instantly and have worked with ever since.

I have also invested heavily in being a part of group programmes myself and have always found they expand my horizons. There is growth in hanging out, even virtually, with business people who are smashing their goals and talking about much bigger numbers than you. People who are ready to help, answer your questions and commiserate with you when you need it is a gift you can give yourself. Hanging around with extraordinary businesswomen has helped me see the blind spots I didn't know I had around success and what is possible.

I appreciate that I am fortunate to live in a city where there are networking opportunities and I understand that isn't the same for every area, although you can be an entrepreneur anywhere now, of course. It is worth looking to see if there are networking opportunities in your area because you never know! If there aren't local face-to-face networking opportunities, remember that online networking is valuable – take a look at the group programmes with Good Girl Rebellion to find your people.

Self-belief and belief in your next move

Your mind is programmed to focus on the negative, the fears that things won't work and you're wasting your time. Yet you have a beautiful creative brain that can imagine a future where all your goals are realised. Making a decision, setting a deadline (with external accountability if you need it) and going all in – this is what successful entrepreneurs do. Are all their decisions the right ones? Of course not. Acting on your ideas will always move you forward. We win or we learn, and both of those things are valuable.

Summary

- A leader is someone who guides the way, who influences, inspires, motivates and acts. It's time for you to define what that means for you.

- Understand who you want to be as a leader. How you already embody that helps show you that you're on your way there.

- Regularly ask yourself where you're holding back and how you're playing small.

- Hyper independence served you in the past, but it's not serving you now. Find ways to get support through hiring staff, collaborating and networking.

- Don't say no to yourself. Ask the question.

- When we collaborate, we become greater than the sum of our parts – the magic happens in the process of working together.

- Learning about running a business and hiring a coach/mentor are ways to guarantee growth.

- It's time to take small steps and bold moves in the right direction.

Conclusion

If I could wave a magic wand, here is what I want for you:

- You are unstoppable and you are limitless. You are so clear on your vision for your business and your life, and you can see it unfolding; it's even better than you dreamt it would be.

- Every morning you can't wait to start your day. You are excited, driven and supremely confident in your ability to craft the success you deserve.

- You know exactly how to manage yourself, building on your strengths, taking bold decisions and matching them with bold action. Imposter syndrome, doubt and indecision no longer affect you; you are focused, clear and in control.

- Your business is thriving, the floodgates are open and sales are pouring in. Your customers/clients are obsessed and can't wait to see what you bring next. Opportunities come to you; they seek you out. You have people working with you who love what they do and are as excited as you are for the future.

- Most importantly, the dream life you've been creating piece by piece is your reality now and sometimes you want to pinch yourself to check that it's not just a dream. It's not.

- You feel deeply grateful, empowered and energised by everything you are building, and you know this is just the beginning.

The fact is, I don't need to wave a magic wand because you are making this your reality.

I want to encourage you to live your life and make your decisions from your hopes, not your fears. This is a decision you need to commit to every day, but it is worth it because the life you craft along the way is more important than the business you grow and the money you make.

You are living in an era of endless possibilities where women have the opportunity to create businesses and make an impact on the global stage. The barriers that once held women back are starting to crumble and it's time to stand up and take up space. You don't need permission, and you don't need a massive audience to build the success you dream of. What you need is clarity, confidence and the willingness to show up for the people who are already looking for what you offer.

Right now, there are people who need exactly what you have to offer – your expertise, your products, your services and your unique voice. They are waiting for you to step forward, to lead and to share your gifts with the world. It's not about chasing followers or hoping to be noticed; it's about deeply connecting with those who truly resonate with you. With the power of technology and digital platforms, you can reach your ideal audience effortlessly, no matter where they are.

You don't have to do it alone; this is just the beginning. It's time to drop your hyper independent identity because it is isolating, keeping you small and holding you back. The fastest way to success is to surround yourself with the right support, guidance and proven strategies that actually work. That's where I come in. Through my coaching and Good Girl Rebellion programmes, I'll help you break through the mindset blocks, self-doubt and hesitation that are holding you back. You'll learn exactly what to do to grow your business, how to do it, and how to become the bold, confident business owner you were meant to be. With expert mentorship, a clear strategy and a community that lifts you up, you'll move faster, achieve more and finally create the business and life you know you're capable of. It's time to start making real progress – because your success isn't just possible, it's inevitable when you have the right support. Let's make it happen together. It would be my privilege to help you along the way. You can find my latest group and one-to-one programmes at goodgirlrebellion/book.

It's decision time. Are you ready for your Good Girl Rebellion? Rebellion is about action; it doesn't come from reading a book. It's not about knowledge, it's about doing. I would much rather you implemented one thing in this book than you digested and memorised it all and did nothing.

It's time to resist the messages of fear and doubt coming from your own mind and do the thing you know you want to do. The life you're dreaming of is on the other side of the action you're afraid to take. Your Good Girl Rebellion is to take that action again and again and again.

Go on, I dare you.

References

1. A Rose, 'The Alison Rose Review of Female
    Entrepreneurship', *HM Treasury* (8 March 2019),
    www.gov.uk/government/publications/the
    -alison-rose-review-of-female-entrepreneurship,
    accessed 22 April 2025
2. Ventureneer, CoreWoman and Women Impacting
    Public Policy, '2025 Report: The Impact of
    Women-Owned Businesses', *Wells Fargo* (2025),
    https://smallbusinessresources.wf.com/wp
    -content/uploads/2025/01/wells-fargo-2025
    -impact-of-women-owned-businesses.pdf,
    accessed 23 April 2025
3. Experian, 'Half of All New Businesses Fail Within
    Three Years of Opening', *Experian PLC* (2023),
    www.experianplc.com/newsroom/press-releases
    /2023/half-of-all-new-businesses-fail-within
    -three-years-of-opening, accessed 23 April 2025
4. G Rubin, *The Four Tendencies: The indispensable
    personality profiles that reveal how to make your life
    better (and other people's lives better, too)* (Harmony,
    2017)

5. TJ Bouchard, DT Lykken, M McGue, NL Segal and A Tellegen, 'Sources of Human Psychological Differences: The Minnesota study of twins reared apart', *Science*, 250/4978 (1990), 223–228, https://doi.org/10.1126/science.2218526

6. R Plomin, JC DeFries, VS Knopik and JM Neiderhiser, 'Top 10 Replicated Findings From Behavioral Genetics', *Perspectives on Psychological Science*, 11/1 (2016), 3–23, www.researchgate.net/publication/292188917, accessed 27 May 2025

7. TM Powledge, 'Behavioral Epigenetics: How nurture shapes nature', *BioScience*, 61/8 (2011), 588–592, https://doi.org/10.1525/bio.2011.61.8.4

8. TJ Bouchard, DT Lykken, M McGue, NL Segal and A Tellegen, 'Sources of Human Psychological Differences: The Minnesota study of twins reared apart'

9. RJ McQuaid, OA McInnis, JDH Stead, K Matheson and H Anisman, 'A Paradoxical Association of an Oxytocin Receptor Gene Polymorphism: Early-life adversity and vulnerability to depression', *Frontiers in Neuroscience*, 9 (2015), 191, https://doi.org/10.3389/fnins.2013.00128

10. A Kogan, LR Saslow, EA Impett, C Oveis, D Keltner and SR Saturn, 'Thin-slicing Study of the Oxytocin Receptor (OXTR) Gene and the Evaluation and Expression of the Prosocial Disposition', *Proceedings of the National Academy of Sciences*, 108/48 (2011), 19189–19192, https://doi.org/10.1073/pnas.1112658108

11. SL Bem, 'Gender Schema Theory and Its Implications for Child Development: Raising

gender-aschematic children in a gender-schematic society,' *Signs: Journal of Women in Culture and Society*, 8/4 (1983), 598–616, https://doi.org/10.1086/493998

12. JS DeLoache, 'Symbolic Functioning in Very Young Children: Understanding of pictures and models', *Child Development*, 62/4 (1991), 736–752, https://doi.org/10.2307/1131174

13. SL Bem, 'Gender Schema Theory: A cognitive account of sex typing', *Psychological Review*, 90/4 (1983), 354–364, www.researchgate.net/publication/232559496, accessed 27 May 2025

14. RA Shweder and MB Sullivan, 'The Cultural Psychology of Gender: Theories and narratives', *Psychological Science*, 4/2 (1993), 86–91

15. BW Roberts, KE Walton and W Viechtbauer, 'Patterns of Mean-Level Change in Personality Traits Across the Life Course: A meta-analysis of longitudinal studies', *Psychological Bulletin*, 132/1 (2006), 1–25, https://doi.org/10.1037/0033-2909.132.1.1

16. SD Pollak and DJ Kistler, 'Early Experience and the Development of Emotional Learning,' *Developmental Psychology*, 38/5 (2002), 749–761, https://doi.org/10.1037/0012-1649.38.5.749

17. International Human Genome Sequencing Consortium, 'Finishing the Euchromatic Sequence of the Human Genome', *Nature*, 431/7011 (2004), 931–945, https://doi.org/10.1038/nature03001

18. S Arnold, K McAuliffe and Y Dunham, 'Gender Differences in Children's Self-Assessment and

Reward Negotiation', *Developmental Psychology*, 61/1 (2025), 1–12

19. EA Locke and GP Latham, *A Theory of Goal Setting and Task Performance* (Prentice-Hall, 1990)

20. EL Deci and RM Ryan, *Intrinsic Motivation and Self-Determination in Human Behavior* (Springer, 1985)

21. J Clear, *Atomic Habits: An easy & proven way to build good habits & break bad ones* (Penguin, 2018)

22. BJ Fogg, *Tiny Habits: The small changes that change everything* (Houghton Mifflin Harcourt, 2020)

23. BF Skinner, *The Behavior of Organisms: An experimental analysis* (Appleton-Century-Crofts, 1938)

24. E Mayo, *The Human Problems of an Industrial Civilization* (Macmillan, 1933)

25. PM Senge, *The Fifth Discipline: The art and practice of the learning organization* (Doubleday, 1990)

26. G Rubin, *The Four Tendencies*

27. EL Deci and RM Ryan, *Intrinsic Motivation and Self-Determination in Human Behavior*

28. G Rubin, *The Four Tendencies*

29. CN Parkinson, *Parkinson's Law, and Other Studies in Administration* (Houghton Mifflin, 1957)

30. International Coaching Federation, 'Global Coaching Client Study' (2009), https:// researchportal.coachingfederation.org /Document/Pdf/abstract_190, accessed 27 May 2025

31. NM Mofokeng and MR Shaw, 'Entrepreneurial Coaching for the Development of

Entrepreneurial Self-Efficacy in Women Entrepreneurs', *IJEBD (International Journal of Entrepreneurship and Business Development)*, 7/2 (2022), 238–245, https://doi.org/10.29138/ijebd .v7i2.2534

32. Kutzhanova, N., Lyons, T.S. and Lichtenstein, G.A., 'Skill-based development of entrepreneurs and the role of personal and peer group coaching in enterprise development.' Economic Development Quarterly, 23(3) (2009), pp.193–210, https://www .researchgate.net/publication/240277419, accessed 27 May 2025

33. M Hartnett, 'The benefit of having an accountability partner as a solopreneur', *Women on Business* (28 January 2021), www .womenonbusiness.com/benefit-accountability -partner-solopreneur, accessed 23 April 2025

34. I Simonson and A Tversky, 'Choice in Context: Tradeoff contrast and extremeness aversion', *Journal of Marketing Research*, 29/3 (1992), 281–295, www.jstor.org/stable/3172740, accessed 27 May 2025

35. K Yu, 'Tall, Grande, Venti: How this brand adapted to market changes without changing its brand identity and original approach', *Valens Research* (24 August 2020), www.valens-research .com/dynamic-marketing-communique/tall -grande-venti-how-this-brand-adapted-to-market -changes-without-changing-its-brand-identity -and-original-approach-monday-marketing -marvels, accessed 24 April 2025

36. B Schwartz, *The Paradox of Choice: Why more is less* (HarperCollins, 2004)

37. SS Iyengar and MR Lepper, 'When Choice is Demotivating: Can one desire too much of a good thing?' *Journal of Personality and Social Psychology*, 79/6 (2000), 995–1006, https://doi.org/10.1037/0022-3514.79.6.995

38. Experian, 'Half of All New Businesses Fail Within Three Years of Opening'

39. P Rozin and EB Royzman, 'Negativity Bias, Negativity Dominance, and Contagion', *Personality and Social Psychology Review*, 5/4 (2001), 296–320, https://psycnet.apa.org/record/2001-09004-002, accessed 27 May 2025

40. PR Goldin, K McRae, W Ramel and JJ Gross, 'The Neural Bases of Emotion Regulation: Reappraisal and suppression of negative emotion', *Biological Psychiatry*, 65/6 (2009), 467–473, https://doi.org/10.1016/j.biopsych.2008.10.004

41. N Doidge, *The Brain That Changes Itself: Stories of personal triumph from the frontiers of brain science* (Viking, 2007)

42. B Katie, *Loving What Is: Four questions that can change your life* (Harmony, 2002)

43. Experian, 'Half of All New Businesses Fail Within Three Years of Opening'

44. S Jeffers, *Feel the Fear and Do It Anyway* (Ballantine Books, 1987)

45. G Mark, *Attention Span: A groundbreaking way to restore balance, happiness and productivity* (HarperCollins, 2023)

46. B Tracy, *Eat That Frog!: 21 great ways to stop procrastinating and get more done in less time* (Berrett-Koehler Publishers, 2001)
47. M Urban, *The Book of Boundaries: Set the limits that will set you free* (Ebury Digital, 2022)
48. D Wallace, *Closed Mouths Don't Get Fed*
49. JB Rotter, 'Generalized Expectancies for Internal Versus External Control of Reinforcement' *Psychological Monographs: General and Applied*, 80/1 (1966), 1–28, https://doi.org/10.1037/h0092976
50. JM Twenge, L Zhang and C Im, 'It's Beyond My Control: A cross-temporal meta-analysis of increasing externality in locus of control, 1960–2002', *Personality and Social Psychology Review*, 8/3 (2004), 308–319, https://pubmed.ncbi.nlm.nih.gov/15454351, accessed 27 May 2025
51. J Blount, *Fanatical Prospecting: The ultimate guide to opening sales conversations and filling the pipeline by leveraging social selling, telephone, email, text, and cold-calling* (Wiley, 2015)
52. A Payne, *Everything You've Been Taught About Sales Is Wrong (*Probably): How to make more sales in a way that feels really good for you (and your clients)* (Authors & Co, 2024)
53. D Wallace, *Closed Mouths Don't Get Fed*
54. D Whitebread and S Bingham, *Habit Formation and Learning in Young Children* (Money Advice Service, 2013)
55. I Yordanova, 'Women in Self-Employment 2020', *The Association of Independent Professionals and the Self-Employed (IPSE)* (2020), www.ipse.co.uk

/campaigns/women-in-self-employment/women-in-self-employment-report, accessed 25 April 2025

56. ZenBusiness, 'The Freelancer Pay Gap', *ZenBusiness Inc* (2 December 2021), www.zenbusiness.com/freelancer-pay-gap, accessed 25 April 2025

57. We-Fi, 'The Case for Investment in Women Entrepreneurs: Advancing gender-inclusive financing and entrepreneurship ecosystems', *Women Entrepreneurs Finance Initiative* (2022), https://we-fi.org/wp-content/uploads/2022/06/We-Fi-Case-for-Investment.pdf, accessed 25 April 2025

58. M Beck, 'The New You: Handling change-back attacks', *Martha Beck*, https://marthabeck.com/2012/10/change-back-attacks, accessed 25 April 2025

59. Experian, 'Half of All New Businesses Fail Within Three Years of Opening'

Further Reading

If you'd like to dive deeper into the subject of personality, check out these books:

Braiker, H, *The Disease to Please: Curing the people-pleasing syndrome* (McGraw-Hill Education, 2001)

Duckworth, A, *Grit: Why passion and resilience are the secrets to success* (Vermillion, 2017)

Funder, DC, *The Personality Puzzle* (WW Norton & Co, 2024)

Moore, DS, *The Developing Genome: An introduction to behavioral epigenetics* (Oxford University Press, 2017)

Plomin, R, Defries, JC, Knopik, S and Neiderhiser, JM, *Behavioral Genetics in the Postgenomic Era* (Worth Publishers Inc., 2012)

Rubin, G, *Better Than Before: What I learned about making and breaking habits* (Crown Publishing Group, 2015)

Acknowledgements

I stand on the shoulders of giants. One of my first jobs was in an independent bookshop and I was tasked with managing the stock of the personal development books. That was nearly thirty years ago, and I continue to have a personal development book addiction. The 'aha' moments that I've got from so many amazing people infuse these pages.

Thank you to Gretchen Rubin, whose *Four Tendencies* work was my first insight into the importance of personality when understanding and managing myself. It stopped me scrabbling around in the dark and started me in the right direction.

To Susan Cain, Glennon Doyle, Elizabeth Gilbert, Gay Hendricks, Regan Hillyer, Ken Honda, Susan Jeffers, Christine Kane, Byron Katie, Austin Kleon, Paul McKenna, Jasmine Manke, Marisa Peer, Daniel

Priestley, Tony Robbins, Robin Sharma, Kasia Urbaniak, Melissa Urban and Chris Voss.

To Jessica Rose, my boss and my friend. I've learnt everything about running a business with integrity from you.

To Anna Payne, my coach and cheerleader. Your guidance and support, particularly when coming up with the REBEL methodology, was invaluable.

To my coach and co-host of the *Full of Ourselves Podcast*, Heidi Hinda Chadwick. I am grateful that the fates brought us together and that we have been on our parallel journeys, pulling each other up when we need it.

To Lynn Powell for so relentlessly supporting artists, including me. The success of Jewellery School Scotland is in our collaboration.

To Jessica Croft, the original Good Girl Rebel and my first coaching client. Thank you for our jewellery collaboration, for beta-reading the book and for being you.

To Martha Beck for all her work, especially her life-changing Wayfinder life coach training.

To my fellow Wayfinder coaches, the AM-Bs. It has been such a gift to be a part of this group of truly astounding people with so much to bring to the world. Alison Ward, BeJay Watson, Bridget Doogan, Courtney Simpson,

Gyongy Szabo, Jen Middleton, Jo van Zwanenberg, Liz Barrow, Melina Faria and Rachel Connor.

To Georgina Nestor, the copywriter with the fearless words.

To my jewellery family: Penny Akester, Alice Cant, Jen Cowdrey, Emily Fletcher, Ann Hassan, Elin Horgan, Sally How, Tori Foster, Hayley Kruger, Emma René, Anna Sweet, Kelly Twigg and Karen Young.

To my family for their unwavering support and love.

To my husband Gary for being you and making me laugh every single day.

The Author

Anna Campbell is an award-winning entrepreneur, business coach and the visionary leader behind the Good Girl Rebellion – a movement empowering high-empathy, high-integrity women to stop building other people's dream businesses and start growing their own.

With a background in psychology, educational technology and life coaching, Anna combines mindset with strategic business mentoring and guidance to help women navigate the leap from start-up to sustainable, quit-your-day-job success. She brings her knowledge from being a key part of building a seven-figure-a-year business and being a certified sales strategist to her one-to-one coaching, group programmes and courses.

Anna is livid about the gender pay gap in self-employ-ment and is campaigning to raise awareness and to support women to charge what they are worth.

As a Wayfinder-certified life coach and former psy-chology lecturer, Anna helps her clients break through limiting beliefs, master their sales confidence and create businesses that align with their values and goals. Her signature blend of coaching and mentorship ensures that women not only grow their businesses but also build lives they truly love.

A sought-after public speaker and podcast guest, Anna is known for her compassionate straight-talking about business growth. Her message is clear: Good Girls don't have to play small. Success isn't about working harder – it's about playing to your strengths and playing to win.

🌐 www.goodgirlrebellion.com

in www.linkedin.com/in/annacampbell
-goodgirlrebellion

📷 @annaccampbell